ON THE MOVE

By the Author of

CENTURY 21
FEAST AND FAMINE
HABITAT
MAN ALIVE
SCIENCE AND SERENDIPITY
SOCIAL MAN

The British military hovercraft passing the Unicorn, a square-rigged vessel. The New York Times.

THE NATURE OF MAN SERIES

5

ON THE MOVE

Man and Transportation

D. S. HALACY, Jr.

MACRAE SMITH COMPANY · *Philadelphia*

MANUFACTURED IN THE UNITED STATES OF
AMERICA
Published simultaneously in Canada by
George J. McLeod Limited, Toronto
7404

Library of Congress Cataloging in Publication Data
Halacy, Daniel Stephen, 1919-
  On the move.

  (The Nature of man series, no. 5)
  SUMMARY: Discusses the advantages and disadvantages of the various means of transportation used by man from prehistory to the present day.
  Bibliography: p.
  1. Transportation—History—Juvenile literature.
  [1. Transportation—History] I. Title.
  TA1149.H34   380.5'09   73-19884
  ISBN 0-8255-4042-9

SE

Contents

ON THE MOVE

CHAPTER
1

On the Move

The world is a great book, of which they who never stir from home read only a page.

Saint Augustine

Biological science is sometimes in doubt as to whether a certain species of life is a plant or an animal. So confusing is the problem that some forms are called "plantimals." There is one simple test, however, that generally separates the plant from the animal: most plants are rooted to the spot; most animals move about. And man is the "movingest" of them all.

Plant life evidently came first. Plants draw energy from the sun and water from the soil, and it is for this reason that they put down roots. Although their trunks, branches, and other parts may move for some distance, the plant as a whole lives in one place through all its existence. Animals gave up this assurance of an energy supply to become rovers, cutting themselves adrift from the soil and roaming the surface of the earth in search of sustenance and other satisfactions.

There was a time when man was a modest traveler, when he might never stray more than a few miles from where he was born. But nature made him a nomad, a follower of food and the weather, sometimes a hunter and sometimes the fleeing prey of other hunters. From their cradle somewhere near the Mediterranean, humans journeyed the thousands of

1

miles down into the African continent, to Europe, Asia, Scandinavia, and finally to the "New World" of North and South America. This, of course, was long before Columbus sailed in search of the Indies and found America.

At first, people relied on legs for travel, their own legs and later those of beasts of burden. Today the horse is still a mount for working cowboys, equestrians, mounted policemen, and polo players. Oxen still pull plows, and elephants haul logs in India. A few "husky" dogs pull Eskimo sleds. But most of us use other, mechanized forms of travel.

Transportation of goods and people led to the wheel and many other great inventions. The boat and the ship were invented for travel across the water—first the rivers and lakes, and then the oceans too. The sail was a transport invention. When the wheel—the circle that rolls so much better than a square—began to roll, it caused the greatest revolution in transportation. No longer would humans or animals have to drag things across the ground. The wheels are still rolling, all over the world.

THE PACE PICKS UP

The first motivation for travel was hunger; early humans moved only as far as was needed to find sufficient food. As time went on, curiosity must have taken over and man went over the next hill to see what was on the other side. Exploration was born of this innate curiosity, and some of the most prominent names in history are those of explorers. There was more to such travels than mere inquisitiveness, of course. Trade was a factor, and so was military conquest. But mankind was born with a need to dream of what lay beyond the hills, beyond the waters, and even beyond Earth itself.

Travel began with a curious human being walking a few miles from his campfire to see what was over the next hill. In this manner we covered much of the habitable dry land of the earth. At water's edge, our kind took to boats and ships and submarines, and now we have explored the seven seas, over their surfaces and as deep as five miles into the great submarine canyons.

When travelers had reached every continent, they fanned out to explore these new opportunities for movement. Ships plied the waterways. Snorting, glowing "iron horses" rolled along twin iron rails from one end of the land to the other, up and down, and back again. More recently, airplanes took to the skies, needing only a mile or so of runway every few hundred miles to take on more passengers and fuel.

When humanity on the move met itself coming back at the far ends of the earth it would seem that transportation had served its ultimate purpose. Such was not the case, as we well know. Having reached the shores of the Pacific Ocean from the original New England colonies, Americans rebounded to the north and south, and into the middle of the country. As their population and supply needs grew, they criss-crossed the land with roads, first of dirt, then of asphalt and concrete. Lately a complex linkage of Federal highways has added its serpentine, multi-level overpass interchanges until there is the real threat of burying urban areas with concrete.

With aircraft man has girdled the earth in every direction until he has begun to run into himself in the sky as he does on the ground. Commercial aircraft regularly fly at altitudes up to eight miles, but even this is not the limit. More recently our astronauts have flown thousands of miles into Earth orbit and then out through deep space to land on the moon. Exploratory robot craft have pushed far past the moon, to Venus, Mars, and beyond, and it is probable that someday human pilots will do the same thing. Already there are human beings who have traveled many millions of miles in their lifetimes. In a single flight of several days' duration, our lunar explorers have traveled through space a distance of more than half a million miles. And those of us still bound to Earth can board an airplane and cover distances of thousands of miles with little thought of the wonder of such a feat.

As recently as 1916, annual travel in the United States

amounted to an average of only 400 miles a year for each person. That was far more than the distance covered by earlier generations, but it was only a hint of what was soon to come. By 1940, the travel average was 2,400 miles a year. Today Americans average 7,000 miles, a distance almost three times the width of our country. An oldtimer would be amazed, but we ourselves are generally shocked that the distance seems so short. Those averages are misleading, for they include the newborn and many others who stay at home. Many of us travel far more than that average figure and cover distances that would take us several times around the world.

Our Biggest Business

Like most developed countries, ours is a nation on wheels— automobile wheels, bicycle wheels, motorcycle wheels, and the heavy wheels of trucks, buses, and trains. We also take to wings, balloons, watercraft, and occasionally even legs to get from here to there in our restless movement up and down and across the land. Nobody seems able or desirous to stay put. We are generally in constant motion, trying desperately to get somewhere, anywhere, including "away from it all," and then turning around and coming home again. The effect is beginning to boomerang. We are being hemmed in on all sides with mazes of freeway and bogged down in traffic jams.

It is easy to get the idea that nobody knows what all the running to and fro is for, what all the milling around is about. Wouldn't the world be a better, quieter place if we all stayed home? Ah, but many of us must travel fifty miles to get to work, and the same distance home again. Some businessmen actually commute thousands of miles to work. Much of the hustle and bustle is a result of our efforts to get away from it all by taking a vacation in the mountains, or back country, or seashore, only to find that half the population has joined us.

Much of the heavy traffic is hauling the goods we need for modern living. The food, gasoline, clothes, appliances and books that are a part of modern living all seem to be manufactured on the other side of the country or halfway around the world. The average American sends or receives 418 pieces of mail per year, adding to the tremendous volume of freight that must be moved by surface, water, or air carriers.

Transportation is America's biggest business; more workers are employed in building automobiles than in raising food. A fourth of our fuel supply is used for transportation. We spend more money for automobiles and other means of getting about than we do for anything else. In the last twenty years America has spent the enormous sum of $2.3 trillion on moving people and goods. In a single year the country spends $200 billion for transportation, twenty percent of the huge total Gross National Product. About three million people in the United States work directly in the transportation industry. Additional millions manufacture equipment used in that industry.

Surface, water, and air are the three basic media for transporting freight and passengers. Surface transportation can be further categorized into rail and highway traffic, the latter consisting of automobiles, trucks, and buses. Highway traffic carries by far the most of the load, both freight and passengers. Trucks account for nearly seventy-five percent of the dollar volume of freight. Railroads carry only about fifteen percent of the total, and waterways the remaining ten percent. Motor vehicles account for even more of the total of passenger traffic. In 1970, automobiles were responsible for nearly $94 billion of the total of $109 billion spent on passenger travel. Airlines, buses, and trains shared the remaining $13 billion, with airlines representing $10 billion of that.

The United States has about 3,750,000 miles of streets and highways, and there are about 115 million motor vehicles registered, nearly nine million of them new cars. There are about 297,000 miles of railroad lines in the United States, traveled by 30,000 locomotives pulling 13,000 passenger cars and nearly 1½ million freight cars, not counting the cabooses! We have more than 29,000 miles of navigable rivers and canals, with 20,000 craft operating on them. There are 16,000 additional vessels traveling in ocean waters, 12,000 airports, of which about 4,500 are public, and about 140,000 miles of federal airways. Airliners number about 2,500, and private aircraft more than 100,000.

So important has transportation become in our world that the United States has found it necessary to establish a Department of Transportation, whose secretary has Cabinet rank. A number of states have followed the lead of the federal government and added similar departments to their administrations. Many authorities say that DOT was far too long in coming and that the problems it must solve in the decades ahead may make it most overworked of all the departments.

THE TROUBLE WITH TRANSPORTATION

Although it is pointed out that there is beginning to be a traffic problem in the more than 1,000 unmanned craft orbiting Earth, billions of dollars of tax money have proved that science can fly men safely to and from the moon. Astronauts travel millions of miles through space with remarkable ease. Yet, back home, there are hopeless snags and jams in local transport. Some residents of urban areas feel trapped there, without personal vehicles and without any efficient kind of urban transit. Some wait in long, smelly lines of traffic in rush hours that grow longer each year. At the beginning of the automobile age, England passed a law that such vehicles could travel no faster than four miles an hour and must be preceded by a man on foot carrying a red flag. Today, some stalled motorists wish they could make even that snail's pace.

There are worse results of vehicular traffic than delay, of course. The most tragic record compiled on our highways is that of fatalities; each year nearly 60,000 die in automobile accidents. A less immediate peril, but still bad news, is the pollution, in a variety of forms ranging from dirty air to noise to defaced landscapes, resulting from the use of the internal combustion engine.

Because of our insistence on "personal mobility" in a system of private ownership and free enterprise, and an increasing necessity for government involvement, the transportation web that laces our society together threatens to strangle us. Part of the problem is the mixture of private and public elements in our various modes of transportation. Cars and trucks are owned by individuals but they operate on public streets and highways. Airlines also are individually owned but they fly from publicly-maintained airports and on airways equipped and regulated by the federal government. Most of our water transport, ocean-going ships, and barges and boats that navigate rivers and canals are privately owned. But they too operate in waterways, ports, and harbors that are public facilities. Rivers and canals are maintained by the U.S. Army Corps of Engineers, and the U.S. Coast Guard maintains maritime law and safety.

In spite of problems they cause, the automobile and the highway it rolls on continue to thrive and are being multiplied with frightening efficiency. There are "paving trains" capable of laying three miles of concrete, twenty-four feet wide, in a single day. The diligent "concrete pouring" has led to loud protests that the highway builders have already paved over an area equal to that of Connecticut, Delaware, Massachusetts, New Hampshire, Rhode Island, and Vermont, with a good start on another state!

Perhaps partly in protest against the woes of mechanized transport, there is a wave of interest in hiking, and backpacking is the new sign of the times. Ironically, however, many of the back-to-nature enthusiasts are to be found along the highways and freeways hitching rides in powered vehicles!

GETTING BACK ON THE TRACK

The development story of transportation is by no means finished but it has reached its most exciting—and trying—phase. Without high-speed transportation, modern society would slow down to a walk. With it, we sometimes seem to be headed for the same fate. The serious problems of pollution, taxation, fuel shortages, and urban transit woes that beset us cry out for solutions that will enlist the best efforts of us all. The younger generation, particularly, will be increasingly plagued by the bad side of a heritage that began with the Baltimore & Ohio locomotive *Tom Thumb,* Henry Ford's wonderful Tin Lizzie, Robert Fulton's paddlewheel *Clermont,* and the frail wood and cloth airplane launched by two bicycle mechanics named Wright.

The future of transportation is perhaps even more exciting than its past. For in that future are such things as 300-an-hour trains riding on a film of air or racing through magnetic rings, electric cars producing no pollution or exhaust of any kind, steam engines that would make James Watt whistle in amazement, and nuclear-powered vehicles. We can look forward to aircraft traveling not at the modest 1,800-mile-an-hour speed of our undeveloped SST, but at a blistering Mach 8 that will fly us anywhere on earth in three hours; to ships that "fly" across the sea; and to submarines that will cruise silently and safely far below the storms that plague surface craft. There may even be subterranean vehicles racing through tunnels bored through solid rock at speeds that will take us anywhere in no more than 42 minutes.

To comprehend such a future it will be useful first to be aware of the past. In the next chapter, then, we will begin at the very beginning, to see where human beings started to take their first steps into the vast world around them.

CHAPTER
2

The Earliest Travelers

Man has been moving about on the earth since our earliest times. At first, however, his movement was slow and he did not cover much distance, except perhaps when forced by such calamities as the ice ages. When he had to travel through rough country from one point to another, he most likely followed the track or trail of animals that had been there far longer than he and over the years had beaten the straightest, firmest, or easiest paths.

Primitive humans were foragers, seeking food suitable for them to eat among the berries, nuts, fruit, grubs, insects, and small animals. Like the animals, people made frequent trips to the nearest waterhole, and like them they needed a safe retreat from weather, wild animals, and hostile humans.

If man had been content with that foraging kind of life, he might still be traveling a limited route from cave to food to water and back again. But humanity was endowed with a drive to do more, a curiosity to see what lay beyond the grove of trees, around the bend, or beyond the mountains. And as the taste for meat grew and people learned more about catching and killing animals, they shifted from foraging to hunting.

Hunting came relatively late in human development, however. Archaeologists have estimated that for at least ninety-five percent of our past we have been food-gatherers. Some small groups of humankind did not progress beyond the food-gathering stage until very recent times, and then only because of the pressure of civilization from outside their world.

Using sticks and stones, primitive food gatherers knocked nuts and fruit from trees, dug up edible roots, and pried shellfish from rocks. Seeds were sometimes harvested from wild grasses. While much food gathered in this fashion was eaten on the spot, gatherers learned to use rude baskets or other containers to carry nuts and seeds home for eating at a later time. And that was the beginning of transportation, the hauling of goods that today is a major industry.

HUNTERS AND FISHERS

Since life must have begun in or near the water, the early people became fishers as well as hunters. Both these supplements to basic food-gathering techniques improved as the slowly increasing population demanded more food, and as human skills and experience increased. Skilled hunting and fishing require more sophisticated equipment than sticks and stones, so invention flourished to produce nets and hooks, spears, clubs, and traps.

Another important change took place as the hunters and fishers began to move ever farther from the safety and familiarity of the cave, the berry vine, and the watering place. From the cradle of civilization, men began to move out in different directions in pursuit of the game they had come to prize for its flavor and in search of the foods required in more abundance by their growing clans and tribes.

Berry pickers seldom rush wildly at their task, and early food gatherers probably moved at a very leisurely pace. But when they became hunters they had to move faster and farther. They learned to move with the stealth of wild animals and to run like the wind in pursuit of food. Humanity was on the move.

In a food-gathering culture, a clan might live in one place all its life and even for several generations, moving only because of some catastrophe like fire, climatic change, or an invasion by more warlike humans or wild animals. Hunters learned that they had to follow their prey as it moved seasonally. They were forced to carry their few possessions with them in their journeys south or north, up into the hills or down into the valleys. Very early in history, human beings became nomads, and we have a heritage of travel tens of thousands of years old. While travel was motivated primarily by practical concerns, there is also a joy in movement that seems a part of the human make-up. It was this ingrained love of travel that Robert Louis Stevenson had in mind when he said "For my part, I travel not to go anywhere, but to go. I travel for travel's sake. The great affair is to move."

In the excitement of the chase, and because of deep-seated human curiosity, primitive hunters often must have become lost in new territory. And so it was necessary to learn the rudiments of navigation, to tell direction by the stars and by the moss on trees, to follow the almost invisible tracks made by animals, and enviously to watch the flight of birds.

Human travel began on the individual's own two legs. Four miles an hour is a good pace, and eight hours of walking is generally enough for anyone in a day. Thus a human being could seldom cover more than thirty miles in a day, even when he had a clear track ahead of him and no swamps, jungles, or wild animals to worry about. Two things extended that range to make man far more a globe trotter. He put animals to use, and he learned to travel on water, first as a floater, and then as a sailor. This dramatic development (which came about much more slowly than it seems in retrospect) made it possible for sea-going humans to travel farther in a few weeks than their land-based cousins could in a lifetime.

On his two legs, or astride an animal, man could and did travel from one end of a continent to another and even from continent to continent across a narrow "land bridge." But water travel allowed him to jump thousands of miles across the oceans and set up new civilizations where man had not been before. It is little wonder that the earliest civilizations based their transportation on the large rivers and seas rather than on roads, for water travel was faster and easier and consumed far less energy. It was no accident that the first great cities were built on or near rivers, canals, or seas.

The First Sailors

While hunters chased their quarry up hill and down dale, fishermen were learning the joys of another, far easier kind of movement. People must have learned early how to swim, aided at first by a branch or log, and tricky currents must have given unexpected rides to such pioneer sailors. Many undoubtedly drowned; others surely were washed ashore miles from where they entered the water, confused, hopelessly lost and unable to return home. But like their land-exploring cousins, early mariners learned how to survive, and eventually how to make the best use of water to get from here to there.

Myths and legends tell of mermen and mermaids and other strange creatures encountered on voyages. Neptune and Poseidon were names given to the sometimes friendly, always unpredictable guardians of the sea. There were early tales and pictures of boys on dolphins. Perhaps some daring early humans did use fish and huge turtles as the first ships. Modern skin divers have learned to hitch rides on whales, sharks, manta rays, turtles, and alligators. But the dangers associated with this kind of water navigation must have been discouraging for all but the bravest. For the average fisherman, a log or some other crude raft had to suffice.

A good swimmer could cross a river or a small lake, diving now and then for shellfish on the bottom. But it was far easier to float leisurely along on a raft. Paddling could be done with the hands or feet, as in swimming, or the craft could be shoved along with a pole or paddled with a board. In that way the current could be assisted, or even overcome, so that return

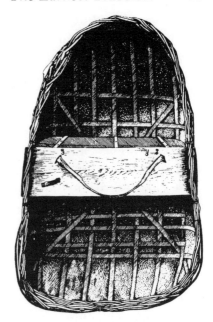

A coracle, a small boat made by covering a wicker or wooden frame with hide, cloth or the like, used by the ancient Britons.

trips could be made by water instead of walking back from a downstream journey.

A great variety of materials served for rafts and boats. Where large logs were not available, fishermen learned to use bundles of reeds. Norwegian archeologist Thor Heyerdahl showed with his experimental voyages on rafts and ships that such craft could be sturdy enough even for ocean crossings. Sometimes sticks and the skins of animals were used to make a vessel that could float. Even the bladders of animals served to good purpose as floats for fish nets and as life preservers for fishermen.

One clever version of such a use was the tying together of two such floats with a short length of rope. The rider sat in the sling between the floats. A modern version of this primitive boat persists today in some countries, where two discarded tin cans are tied together with rope. Leonardo da Vinci invented a primitive "scuba" outfit of this kind, suggesting that bladders could not only serve as waterwings but even furnish breathing air in case the user became submerged!

Because a boat of wood or other perishable material leaves few traces for archeologists to find, we cannot be positive about the age of this means of travel. However, it seems sure that boats were in use more than 6,000 years ago, and that 5,000 years ago elaborate sailing craft were making long journeys carrying many people and tons of goods.

Early sailors learned by accident to use the currents to move their craft. They also learned to make ferries cross rivers in each direction, using vines for ropes. And sometime during those early maritime days some unsung pioneer used a sail to harness the power of the wind.

Winds blew then as now, and it must have blown rafts and dugout canoes across the water. Perhaps some genius realized that as he stood up, the wind pushed his craft along faster, and that if he spread his cloak, he could go faster yet! The next step would be a separate sail; and further refinements would come as sailors learned to rig the sail and set it for different purposes. It must have seemed a miracle when sailors learned that they could actually sail against the wind by patiently tacking back and forth toward their goal.

The earliest long journeys must have been by water. We know to a certainty that primitive humans sailed thousands of miles across the open Pacific in rude craft on trips that today tax the skill and courage of sailors in far better craft and with the advantage of several thousand years of maritime science and technology.

ANIMAL POWER·

There is an old saying that "If wishes were horses, beggars would ride." Before people invented riding, they traveled on land exclusively by "shank's mare," as our legs used to be called. When it was necessary to carry a load, the first pack animal was a man—or, more likely, a woman! After human beings began to war amongst themselves, it became the practice to take captives, and some of them became slaves, performing hard tasks like hauling loads. Before feeling sorry for such human packhorses, we must remember that they were probably the lucky ones; the less fortunate victims were eaten.

Early man was a frail little creature compared with many wild animals of his time. Humans had no horns, fangs, or claws, and until they developed weapons they fled from all but the small animals they sought for food. To early humans, the idea of using a horse or some other animal for transportation would have made about as much sense as our trying to ride a panther. The first use of animal energy in transport came in a roundabout way, as many revolutionary developments do.

Another old saying tells us man's best friend is the dog. Other pet lovers might argue about that, but the dog surely is our oldest animal friend. The way this came about is interesting and touching. Some animals owe their beginnings to superstition and religious meaning. The cat is an example. Early Egyptians attached supernatural significance to the cat, which is still a most popular pet in much of the world. However, the dog and man seem to have come together simply because they liked one another; they got along well. Ancient legends of peoples still not far past the Stone Age culture tell of how the first dog came to a primitive tribe, was fed by them, and then enticed another dog to join him. Their pups became even more domesticated, and man and dog began the association that has strengthened in the thousands of years since then.

, Dogs joined in early hunts; they still serve this purpose. And dogs seem also to have become the first pack animals. Not that they were big enough for any but small children to ride, but they carried and pulled loads men were tired of pulling. The primitive Indians of North America lived in tents, and when in their nomadic existence the time came to move on, they bundled up the tent, poles and all, and tied the poles to camp dogs, who dragged them along the trail to the next campground. This was undoubtedly hard on the dogs, but the Indians had no horses (and would not until the Spanish explorers brought them from Europe) and had not domesticated elk or deer or buffalo. Farther north, the Eskimos used dogs to pull loads too. The husky is well known in the lore of the north country. Similar use of dogs prevailed in Asia and Northern Europe.

Early in his carnivorous career, man tracked down and killed game animals in their natural wild habitat. But man is never satisfied. He began to wonder, over the thousands of years, about all that wasted motion on his part. First he had to go out and find the animals. Next he had to kill them, often a very dangerous process involving the risk of death or injury for the hunter. Then he had to haul the meat back to wherever his camp was. Slowly, and again in very indirect ways, the domestication of animals evolved.

Man sometimes ate his friend the dog, but that was generally only in emergency situations. The idea of domesticating such animals as reindeer, cows, and sheep took time to develop. A step along the way might have been the early superstitions that preceded religion. Primitive humans believed there were supernatural spirits in certain animals—bears for example—that could give magical power to their captors. So these animals were captured and kept in special cages or pens. That custom was the forerunner of the zoo. The fierce "totems" must have been objects not only of awe but great interest, particularly to young people in the tribe.

Perhaps the animals were sacrificed, and the food eaten. Not only did the rite have superstitious significance, but the meat proved to be tasty. Slowly the idea came of keeping a meat supply close at hand, in a pen, or placidly grazing on a nearby hill. Sheep were among the first animals to be so domesticated. In the north, reindeer provided meat, milk, and a bonus of hides, bones, and other raw materials needed in the local economy.

Thus, animals served man in a variety of ways. He used their tracks to find his way when he traveled. The animals provided food for him, and slowly they began to serve as beasts of burden too. Oxen could pull plows no man or woman could drag through the hard ground. And oxen could haul immense loads that would stagger a man. Even the smaller ass could carry a good load, make fair speed, and be handled easily by a human leader or a rider.

People were weary of carrying heavy loads and of walking the hot and dusty or cold and icy trails of their forefathers. Mothers habitually carried their children along the trail; in rare cases a sick or injured adult might also be carried on a human back. Slowly it dawned on some men that there was little reason to walk when they could ride.

Surely there must have been diehard traditionalists who frowned at this new fad that would surely weaken the moral fiber and the physical strength of humankind. If walking was good enough for the chiefs of old, it would do for them; those weak enough to give in to riding an ox or a donkey would come to no good end. Bearing out this belief were the many spills taken by early riders, spills that could cause broken bones and sometimes death. The excitement of today's rodeos may give an idea of the catastrophes that sometimes resulted from early riding attempts. In those times saddles, bridles, and reins were unknown. It is believed that man began to use the larger animals for pack-carrying and for riding somewhere about 5,000 B.C. If so, the cowboy has a heritage some seven thousand years old.

Today we design vehicles to handle our transportation tasks. Early human beings were stuck with the animals they found in the wilds about them. Yet they were able to improve on that situation as time went on. Through selection, they allowed certain animals to flourish and to develop in certain directions. Early cows, for example, were huge, wide-horned monsters terribly difficult to domesticate. But over thousands of years, breeders produced animals with characteristics more suitable for the jobs that needed to be done.

FARMING: A TRANSPORTATION REVOLUTION

Hunting made man far more a traveler and transporter than he had been in the food-gathering economy; it caused the first travel revolution. Surprisingly, an even greater change in habits came with the practice of agriculture.

Just as people learned the value of domesticating their meat supply, they slowly came to realize the benefits of cultivating plants. Farming must have come about by accident in many places, when seeds brought in by foragers sprouted near camp. It is difficult now to believe that the practice of agriculture did not spread like a forest fire as soon as one group practiced it. Instead, the growth was slow. In fact, there are still some people who do not farm but subsist entirely by foraging, hunting, and fishing. Farming skills must have been discovered and lost again many times before that occupation became widespread enough to have broad effect on human society. But eventually, and roughly about the same time as the domestication of animals, agriculture was established in the Near East and perhaps in parts of China. Researchers tell us that Iraq (Mesopotamia in ancient times) was one of the earliest sites of animal and plant domestication; perhaps about 12,000 years ago these revolutions got started.

If hunting and fishing made man more mobile, it would seem likely that domestication of his food supply would make him less inclined to rove far and wide. At first this was probably true, and yet the agricultural revolution led to even more moving about—led in time to the settling of most of the world's lands and to the exploration of the depths of the ocean, and even of the moon.

This remarkable fact requires some explanation. As anyone who has tried to subsist on berries knows, foraging is just about a full-time job. The hunter is always busy chasing his quarry, killing it, or taking care of his catch between kills. Just staying alive was a full-time human occupation before the domestication of animals and the development of agriculture. Then, for the first time, a family could put by sufficient food not just for themselves but for a few more people besides. As farming has improved in the developed countries, we have seen the ratio of farmers to those in other occupations decrease to the point that now it is fairly accurate to say that one farmer can feed fifty or more people. Those fifty people can do something else, of course. And part of that something else is traveling about in a variety of vocations that were impossible before the leisure and surplus that farming provided.

Early man provided his own food, made his own clothes, and was his own religious leader and teacher. When he finally had more food than he needed, he became a specialist in clothes or footwear, a spearmaker, or even an artist. Relatively soon after the domestication of the food supply came trading. And trading grew to include travel. The "amber trade" was a big business thousands of years ago; amber is hardened tree resin that men took a fancy to as jewelry. In our own country the Indians living along the California coast traded seashell jewelry with Indians from inland. Other trading materials were *lapis lazuli* (a blue gem stone), flint for weapons and tools, ivory, gold, animal hides, silk, jade, lacquerware, spices, and even human slaves.

ROADS TO TRAVEL ON

There was no Parcel Post in those days, so the artisan had to "get on the road" periodically. In time a new occupation sprang up, that of trader. While the expert artisan designed and created more jewelry, the skilled trader could be marketing the finished wares for a better price than the unbusinesslike artist was likely to obtain—and the trader was probably getting more money than the artist! In time traders began to hire "drovers" or teamsters to do the actual hauling. Kings did the same thing, to bring precious stones and

minerals from their distant mines, or ice from the moun-
taintops to cool desserts for their feasts.

In time, empires grew, and much travel was necessary for
keeping in touch with farflung holdings. Armies were created
to protect the empires from nomadic invaders who lurked in
the outlands. Religion grew, and an army of priests and clerks
and scribes were paid out of surplus production. Shrines were
built, and much travel developed—and continues—in the
form of pilgrimages to the holy places. The Holloway or Har-
roway Road in England is believed to have derived its name
from the Old English words *hearg-weg* for the "shrine way"
leading to Stonehenge.

An animal frequenting a water hole gradually beats down a
trail. Man's first roads were these narrow trails, gradually
widened to a track or "trace" through the grass. As humans
prospered and increased in numbers, they made their own
trails and gradually improved them. Some of the roads, even
the early ones, seem remarkable to us today.

A CART FOR THE HORSE

While it might seem likely that paved roads would come
only after wheeled vehicles were developed, this was not
true in the "New World." There the Incas and Mayas built
hundreds of miles of stone roads that were great engineering
accomplishments and helped to produce a fairly advanced
civilization with excellent communication and a system of
inns for travelers. Neither South Americans nor North Americans invented the wheel. In its place, the North American Indians developed the *travois*, probably from their folded tents
and poles—simply by tying two poles to either side of the
dog, and later the horse, with the other ends dragging on the
ground.

Farther north, the Eskimos developed the sledge, or sled, as
it had been developed in Europe, Asia, and even in Africa. In
the frozen north country, over ice and snow, the sled runner
far excels the wheel in efficiency, of course, and skis were a

logical development in place of roller skates! Observing the better operation of runners on snow or ice, teamsters in dry country learned to lubricate their runners with water, and even with milk and butter, which were the forerunners of lubricating oils to be used later when machines were developed.

So people had boats to carry them great distances on water. They had pack and riding animals ranging from the donkey to the elephant (which has carried everything from teak logs in Asia to Hannibal's army in Europe). Some people were beginning to hitch their animals to crude vehicles, in which loads were pulled far more efficiently than they could be carried. It was time for the next great invention in transportation—the wheel.

CHAPTER
3

Wheels; and Roads to Roll Them On

Today it seems to be wheels that make the world go round. All about us are wheels—on automobiles in garages and on bicycles, tricycles, and wagons in yards. Watches are full of wheels, and so are the washing machines, driers, and air-conditioners. Even the telephone dial is a wheel, and so are door knobs, and radio and telephone dials. We speak of "wheeling and dealing," and "having wheels" is important to most of us. An important person is a "big wheel" and songs have been written about the "wheel of fortune." Take away the wheel and life would be vastly different from what we are used to.

It is hard to accept the fact that the North American Indians did not have wheels when white men came to the continent; neither did the Mayas or the Incas, despite their otherwise advanced society. There are still peoples today who do not make use of the wheel. It is claimed that one reason for the slow realization of the wheel's uses is that there is no counterpart for it in nature. Living creatures are to some extent machines, using levers, pumps, valves, push-pull mechanisms, and even switches and amplifiers. But there are no wheels in us, despite cartoons of wheels going around in our heads.

Perhaps this is a valid reason for not discovering the wheel, actually classed as one of the simple machines. It is just a lever wrapped in a circle. Earth forms a huge fat wheel, rotating on its axis as it spins through space and about the sun.

Primitive inventors may be forgiven for not knowing that Earth was round. However, tree trunks are round too, and surely the ancients observed the ability of logs to roll across the ground or down a hill. In cold countries, primitive children may have made big snowballs and rolled them downhill, as we do today. In snow a wheel is of little use, however, and skis and sleds were much more practical means of getting over the slippery stuff.

Fire was put to use by man long before the wheel, but in his tools for making fire he used the principle of the wheel and still does. One early fire starter was the "fire drill," a shaft rotated between the palms or with a bow or other device to create frictional heat for kindling a fire. The rolling of the fire drill shaft across the palms is like that of a wheel across the ground. In addition to fire drills, humans made use of boring tools and sockets on such devices as spear heads, spinning wheels, and door hinges long before putting the wheel to use on vehicles.

Hollowed logs were undoubtedly among the first boats, coming long before wheeled vehicles. The boat builders must have found it easy to transport these primitive craft to the water's edge by rolling them along the ground—an ironical case of not being able to see the wheel for the trees! Today it is difficult to see how the useful principle of rolling objects could have gone undeveloped for so long. Fire and log "canoes" were probably used hundreds of thousands of years before the wheel appeared, sometime around 3500 B.C.

THE POTTER'S WHEEL

It is obvious that the wheel developed in about the same place that domestication of animals and agriculture did. Evidence suggests that the first wheeled vehicles probably appeared in what is now Iraq. At about the same time—or perhaps just after—the wheel was first used in another capacity.

Agriculture created a need for more than vehicles. Crude baskets had served for carrying loads for some time, but such baskets were not ideal for carrying water or for cooking. Some crude stone vessels were made, and they served the purpose, but potters learned to make vessels much more quickly and in greater variety by shaping clay and then firing it to make it hard and durable.

Few pots are square or triangular. Round pots came naturally, and an artisan could make passably good ones free hand. But human beings are never satisfied, and perhaps also a litte lazy; there is always someone looking for a better way to do things. Perhaps the profit motive was a factor, too, in the dawning age of trade and the specialization of labor. At any rate, the potter's wheel evolved. "Throwing" pots was a faster, more accurate method of making them, and by about 3500 B.C. that handy use of the wheel seems to have become widespread.

Many archeologists believe that the agricultural revolution also led to the use of wheel. Before it became necessary to haul quantities of food to town (and possibly to haul manure from town to farm) there was little need for wheeled transport. The boat and the sailing ship developed as a result of fishing, which long antedated farming, of course. These craft served not only for fishing but also, to a limited extent, for exploration. The first cities were built near water, and it was boats and ships that were first put to use for transport. However, they could not do all of the work, and the need grew for a more efficient land transport system than loading goods onto oxen or donkeys. Slowly the drivers learned that there was a good way to carry more. So the cart came after the horse. And, surprisingly, it came before the wheel.

The remains of sledges that must have been built before 5000 B.C. have been found in Northern Europe. Loads were dragged about on slick runners fairly efficiently except through mud or other very difficult terrain. The sledge was ideal for snow and ice, and until the snowmobile its use persisted in northern lands.

away for firewood and paving stones were taken as building material. It was many centuries before civilization recovered sufficiently to build new roads, but they fell far short of the old Roman models.

Nevertheless, road travel went on, and laws continued to be passed. In 900 A.D. King Alfred passed a law that a "far-coming man or a stranger journeying through a wood or on a highway" must shout or blow a horn or be held as a thief to be either killed or held for ransom. There was good reason for this fierce punishment.

"Highwaymen," as they came to be called, were robbing and murdering travelers. Such criminals had begun their trade back in the later days of the Roman roads but had been put down for a time by the soldiers. Now they were back in force, including such romantic figures as Robin Hood.

Before 1300, Europeans found it necessary to pass laws for the removal of trees lining the roads so that robbers could not hide there. Legend has it that even that precaution did not stop them, and a defense technique adopted by victimized travelers was the reason for Europe's custom of driving on the left side of the road. Drivers took to driving close along the left side of the roadway and defending themselves against robbers with a sword in their right hand, for the robbers had to come from that side. The American practice of driving on the right is said to come from early travel in Conestoga wagons, the prairie schooners that moved settlers west. The left front ox was the lead animal, and on meeting another wagon, the driver dismounted and walked alongside that animal. It was handier to keep to the right when passing a team going the other way.

COMING OF THE TURNPIKE

Having finally recovered from the long disruption of the Dark Ages, European civilization forged ahead again. Roads and vehicles took on greater importance. It has been humorously noted that the situation must have really been terrible, for one of England's pioneer road builders named John Metcalf was better known as Blind Jack. He actually had been blind since he was six years old. Cobblestone roads made their appearance; some still exist. Men like McAdam and Telford returned engineering science to roadbuilding, and transportation profited from their work. Indeed, Telford was nicknamed the "Colossus of Roads." The ancient city of Antioch had lighted its streets as early as A.D., 450 using tar lanterns; by 1700 English coachmen lighted their vehicles as a further aid to night driving.

Passenger traffic was frowned on for a long time. Some government leaders called the practice laziness and warned against it, but the condition of the roads was probably a greater deterrent to travel. Many of them were terrible. A joke popular at the time was the one about a man with a wooden leg who turned down a ride in an English coach: He said he was in a hurry.

One critic said that since stagecoaches were forever getting stuck in the mud, why not abolish them, and then there would be no need for roads or coaches! A better solution was the "turnpike," or privately built toll road. The odd name comes from the wooden barrier, studded with pikes or sharp sticks, that prevented passage until the toll was paid. With these better roads coaches could make great speed between cities and towns. Many blamed the turnpike and coach for bringing more and more people to the city, for who would then want to go back to the farm after having seen great London?

THE BICYCLE: PERSONAL WHEELS

A popular vehicle in some Asian countries is the "pedicab," or three-wheeled passenger vehicle pedaled by its driver. This pollution-free public transit system is a cross between the "rickshaw," invented in 1871 by an American missionary in the East named Jonathan Gobel, and the bicycle, invented somewhat sooner by many people.

The "Draisine" or hobby-horse, c 1818.

Man traveled on land first on his own legs, "shank's mare," then on animals. Later he hitched animals to wheeled vehicles. The idea of riding on wheels *without* an animal came to flower in about 1800, although drawings found in ancient Egypt and in Pompeii seem to suggest the existence or possibility of such wheeled vehicles. A stained glass church window at St. Giles in England dating from 1580 shows an angel riding what looks like a scooter bike.

The first practical bicycle came in the form of the *celerifere*, a French invention consisting of two wheels, a seat, and a crude handlebar. The contraptions had no pedals or steering equipment, but they went like a streak down hills. By 1818 Germany had contributed the steerable "Draisine," which England imported and called everything from a velocipede to a hobby horse. The inventor of the Draisine was German Baron Karl von Drais, chief forester for the Grand Duke of Baden. Von Drais was able to push himself along on wheels about four times as fast as he could walk.

In 1838 an Englishman named Macmillan added pedals to the vehicle, but strangely the idea did not catch on for a long time. Next came tricycles that were harder to tip over, and then the ungainly "highwheelers" with pedals attached directly to the front wheel. Slowly the smaller "safety bicycles" came into style, with a drop frame for ladies. Pneumatic tires were added, along with gears and chain, and by 1895 hundred-mile bike races were common. One such race in New England was won by a woman entrant. Later a male cyclist pedaled at the fantastic speed of seventy-six miles an hour. Tandems and bicycles built for two, three, and even ten appeared, and bicycle clubs sprang up everywhere. And it was bicyclists who agitated for better roads. Today we see a renewed interest in bicycling—and a new clamor for better bike paths.

The bicycle was one of the most remarkable wheeled vehicles to appear in civilization. Inexpensive and light in weight, it could be ridden by just about anyone. It required no fuel and produced no pollution, making it better on two counts than the horse it replaced in some instances. A generation of telegram messengers, postmen, and ice-cream peddlers made their rounds astride two- or three-wheelers; In World War I the bicycle was even used to good advantage as a light scouting vehicle.

The time was ripe for the next great jump in transportation, the addition of the engine to the wheel. Men had produced wheels, roads, and even rails, for there were now some horse-drawn railroads and streetcars that ran on tracks. A variety of mechanical engines were doing tasks that once required animal—sometimes human—muscles. Now it was time to put all these various inventions together. The locomotive and the automobile would write the next chapters in the story.

CHAPTER
4

The Coming of Engines

Until the industrial revolution in the seventeenth century, people used two kinds of energy in getting from Point A to Point B. They harnessed animal energy, the muscles of humans or of a variety of animals. And they used the energy of the sun. The latter seems like a remarkable statement until we look at it in more detail. The first travel by means other than walking was most likely floating down a stream, using water power. Later, the power of the wind was made to drive boats and ships across bodies of water even including the great oceans. Waterpower and windpower are both produced by the heat energy of the sun.

Solar heat evaporates water on the surface of the earth, and rising air currents lift the vapor to where it forms clouds. These in turn drop rain, snow, or hail back to earth and this precipitation makes the rivers that flow downstream in response to the pull of gravity. Some air currents caused by the heating of the sun are horizontal—the wind currents that could drive ships, windmills, and even "wind wagons."

In its basic form, energy is heat. A fuel produces heat; man and the animals eat food and convert this "fuel" to power for their daily activities. That food was produced from the heat energy of the sun. The "fossil" fuels, coal, oil, natural gas, and wood, were also produced directly from the heat energy of the sun and have stored that energy for hundreds of millions of years. Even fuels must be converted to heat to produce power.

We depend on continuous production from farms and ranches for food; there is no big stockpile of it somewhere to mine, although there is a small supply in canned and frozen foods that would last a short time. Our food supply is "income," and, until the industrial revolution, mechanical power for industry and transportation also depended on income sources such as animals, wind, and water.

Humans harnessed fire hundreds of thousands of years before the invention of agriculture, the domestication of animals, and vehicular travel. Fire kept people warm, drove off wild creatures, cooked food, and sometimes cleared and fertilized fields for producing food. The realization that fire could also do mechanical work was very slow in coming, and not until the time of the Greek scientist Hero did anyone seriously consider using heat for power. In about A.D. 50, Hero built and demonstrated a primitive heat engine called the *aelophile*, which may have been used in religious services to open and close altar doors. However, the Greeks studied science for its own sake rather than for practical use, and the aelophile remained merely a curious device of no practical value.

THE STEAM ENGINE

Inventors and engineers were so taken up with boats and ships, wagons, chariots, windmills, waterwheels, and the like that it was not until the seventeenth century that they rediscovered the steam engine. French, Italian, and German experimenters demonstrated such things as a steam pump that actuated a garden fountain, a modernized *aelophile* that was a forerunner of today's turbine engines, and a vacuum so strong that horses could not pull apart the two metal hemispheres enclosing it.

Not until late in the century did Denis Papin, of France, do something more practical. This clever inventor produced the pressure cooker. He was less successful when he built a paddle-wheel steamboat, for the boatmen chased him out of town with their oars. However, the idea of using steam to produce power had taken hold at last, and helping it along was the growing need for better ways to pump water from ever-deepening coal mines. Running out of wood for fires for industrial forges and for other uses, the English had taken to coal, even though some called it the "Devil's brimstone" and worried about the pollution it created. The first working steam engine was designed in 1663 by the Marquis of Worcester while he was serving a prison term on political charges. Called a "water commander," that crude ancestor of the steam engine was actually a huge pump driven by steam from a coal-fired boiler. It worked, but it was a clumsy device that required much effort to open and close its valves.

Mine owners continued to use horses to pump their mines until 1698, when Thomas Savery patented a more workable steam pump that he called the "Miner's Friend." He began to sell his product to mine operators as a substitute for horsepower.

That was thirty-eight years before the birth of James Watt, the man generally credited with inventing the steam engine. Another inventor named Newcomen teamed up with Savery and the two produced a much-improved engine fitted with a moving piston. According to legend, the first automatic operation of the engine came about when a clever apprentice who had been hired to move the valves by hand simply tied ropes to their ends so they could move themselves.

A century or so after the Marquis of Worcester invented his stream beds became blocked with factories there was no popular device and improved it greatly. He boosted engine efficiency about fourfold (still achieving only about 4 percent efficiency, nevertheless, and added such refinements as rotating wheels, which would lead before long to another revolution. Watt also developed the system of rating engines by "horsepower."

The steam engine was gradually adopted by industry for mines, mills, forges, and machine tools previously operated by animal power, manpower, wind, and waterpower. As stream beds became blocked with factories there was no room for more millwheels. Like the mines, industrial plants needed another power source. Along with power, the steam engine produced heat, noise, and pollution. Many people objected, but the number of machines steadily increased and the coal miners continued to prosper by selling coal to fuel them.

STEAM GOES TO SEA

Almost as soon as Denis Papin had put together a steam engine, he tried to drive a boat with it. For a variety of reasons, his was a premature attempt, but it was inevitable that others would pursue the idea. An engine that could pump water, hammer metals, and operate the air bellows of a forge could probably row a boat. Before long, the steam engine was uprooted from its stationary mounting and installed in a variety of vehicles. As early as 1790 a man named John Fitch sailed a steamboat in America, and even he was a latecomer to the steamboat scene. In fact, the paddlewheel boat idea had long been ready and waiting for steamboat builders.

In A.D. 372 a Roman writer had described a fighting ship driven by ox-powered paddlewheels, an idea that seems to have been adopted from the floating grain mills that were in use even earlier. If the flow of current past a barge could drive a waterwheel on the barge, why not turn the wheel by some means and drive the barge across the water?

In 1736, two years before James Watt was born, Jonathan Hulls in England built and operated a steam-powered tugboat in the Thames River, using a Savery engine. It would seem that fame and fortune would be assured for Hulls, whose name was most appropriate for boat designing. But he was doomed to ridicule and failure, and another steamboat builder died of apoplexy in England about that time.

John Fitch never did use the conventional paddlewheel system. First he used a kind of caterpillar tread like those snowmobiles use to traverse snowy terrain. Then he used crank-driven oars, and finally he invented the screw propeller that today drives nearly all vessels. Another American invented a jet-propelled craft that took water in at the bow and ejected it from the stern, a very advanced idea. Yet with all this demonstration of inventive genius, the consensus of the scientific world was that there was no hope for steamboats. Indeed, as late as 1803 the Philosophical Society of Philadelphia, including brilliant men like Benjamin Franklin, stated flatly that steam navigation was impossible, even setting down six reasons why.

There are such things as an idea's being ahead of its time, or people's not being ready for progress. John Fitch finally committed suicide. He was depressed not because his boat had failed but because even though he operated it successfully on a regularly scheduled run, only a few people paid any attention. Early steamboats were clumsy craft, of course. Engines of that time were designed to remain in one place forever and were built like forts. Transplanting such a monster into a boat was difficult, and potential financial backers were put off by the apparent danger of frequent explosions, fires, and breakdowns. Even when successful, steamboats were slower than sailboats or muscle-powered craft. Spectators often yelled suggestions that the craft should be converted into a grist mill.

Ship navigation was of course popular and important at that time. Great waterways were being dug, including the wonderful Erie Canal, which cut shipping costs to a fraction of what they had been. But it was sailing vessels or barges, which floated with the current or were drawn by teams of horses along the bank, that carried goods and passengers. A steamboat that could make a speed of two or three knots would drift *backward* in a swift river current, even though it could make good speed traveling with the current. A better vessel was needed, and not until Robert Fulton was one available.

Fulton was a remarkable man. He was a noted portrait painter, and he invented a submarine, the *Nautilus*, that inspired the writing of Jules Verne's *Twenty Thousand Leagues Under the Sea.* Yet for the *Clermont* (better known as *"Fulton's Folly"*), he noted that "there was never an encouraging word from anyone." Only when in 1807 he sailed the *Clermont* on a long trip up and down the Hudson River at an average speed of five knots did the age of steamboats finally arrive.

POWER FOR THE RAILROADS

A steamboat could be a sizable affair, so engine weight was not a critical factor on the water. Not surprisingly, steam power in land vehicles was an even harder proposition. The first success came on the railroads, perhaps because all the essentials were there before the development of the steam engine.

The idea of a *railroad* was not new. In the early sixteenth century in Europe, ore was hauled from mines in cars that moved along wooden tracks, using animal power, manpower and sometimes, unfortunately, child power. Some tunnels were so low that only children could move through them. The famed Newcastle coal mines in England used wooden track for their ore cars as early as 1602. A century later, about the

Horse-tram used at Newcastle-upon-Tyne. 1773.

only improvement was the substitution of iron track. Hauling was still done by animals, and animals were still used to pump the water from mines.

In 1826, nearly twenty years after Fulton's success with the *Clermont*, the first railroad was introduced in America. That short line in New England hauled only freight, including the stone for building Bunker Hill Monument. It was powered by horses. The great Baltimore & Ohio inaugurated its service in 1830, carrying passengers thirteen miles in one hour and fifteen minutes, still with horses. Oliver Evans, a pioneer industrial engineer, had built an ungainly "amphibian" steam craft in 1805. Fitted with paddlewheels, it could move on land or water, but not very well on either. Not until 1828 did the locomotive *Tom Thumb* make a test run against a conventional horse team—and it lost the race.

The first steam locomotive seems to have been the product of Richard Trevithick of England, in about 1800. By 1829 George Stephenson was running his *Rocket* at such fantastic speeds that alarmists began to spread wild scare stories: Human beings could not stand the strains that would be caused by traveling at 30 miles an hour. Their breath would be taken away, and their blood would boil!

Further handicapping the development of railroads were ridiculous laws, probably passed by stagecoach and carriage interests. Perhaps the worst was that no steam vehicle could travel faster than four miles an hour, and each one had to be preceded by a signalman walking ahead of it, carrying a red flag by day and a lantern by night! Of course the noise primitive steam vehicles made and the danger of boiler explosions alarmed the man in the street. Added to restrictive laws were high taxes and tolls levied on the new form of transportation. As a result, the railroads developed very slowly, taking decades instead of being adopted immediately, as it would seem they should have been. The problems were many. Economics, legal questions, selfish interests, and fear of "infernal machines" all slowed the coming of powered vehicles.

Robert Fulton's *Clermont* looked as if she had been built by a man who knew little about mechanics and less about a ship, but on the Hudson in 1807 she was the world's first steamer in regular commercial service.

The first passenger locomotive, 1808.

But they finally came, of course. George Pullman and his luxurious Pullman cars that even provided sleeping arrangements for train travelers offered a new era of transportation. It was largely the railroads that opened the American west to settlement. A century and more ago, railroad lines linking the east and west met in the midwest, and a golden spike was driven to commemorate the event. In time the railroads even retired the thousand and more Mississippi River steamboats and many of the canal ships and barges as well. After the conventional railroads came the subways and elevated trains, the streetcars, trolleys and cable cars.

In the heyday of railroading, the height of prestige was to own a private railroad car. Most of the wealthy had them, and there are still a few people today who cling to this old custom. But there was another development coming that would change much of the world's travel habits. Up to that point, nearly all powered transport was public rather than private. Even if a man owned a railroad car he was limited to the railroad company's tracks and schedules. There was "personal transport" too, but only behind a team of horses. What was wanted and needed was a private powered vehicle. The automobile would completely change our society.

THE AUTOMOBILE: POWER FOR THE PEOPLE

We take the automobile for granted today and have for many years. It is difficult to think of a time when it was not available, but that is because hindsight is generally better than foresight. Until about two hundred years ago, a carriage that would travel without being pushed or pulled by man, animal, or wind was in a class with the magic carpet. It became possible only with the invention of engines.

In 1769 a Frenchman named Nicholas Cugnot built a three-wheeled carriage that needed no horses to move it along the road. In place of a team of animals, it mounted a huge, smoking steam boiler. In appearance it was much like an old-fashioned steamroller, and it probably weighed about as much. Unfortunately it did not go nearly as fast as a steam-roller, moving along only about two miles an hour. Actual speed was difficult to determine, however, since it was impossible to keep it running for an hour. To make things more difficult, a mob of angry farmers once beat and stoned poor Cugnot for frightening their animals. With all these obstacles, only the most dedicated "steamwagon" enthusiasts operated such monstrosities, gritting their teeth when they were passed at great speed by a horse and carriage that cost a fraction as much and would not blow up or otherwise frighten citizens or livestock.

While we tend to think that great inventions are always eagerly snapped up, this did not happen at all. Only a handful of brave men like the House brothers of Bridgeport, Connecticut, and France's Amedee Bolée kept putting together their lumbering steam wagons and risking life and limb to drive them about. The coming of the automobile was a long, slow process.

A century after Cugnot's turtlelike steam wagon, Thomas Rickett of Buckingham, England, was building a steam-driven private carriage seating three people including the driver and capable of speeds up to 12 miles an hour. He had moved the steam engine to the rear, providing much better visibility for passengers. By 1866, H. P. Holt was operating a steam carriage seating nine and traveling 20 miles an hour on level roads. Yet even after more than a hundred years of development, personal self-propelled vehicles were not taking the country by storm. Steam itself was still one of the reasons. In addition to dangers of fire and explosion, the engine had the disadvantage of being slow to fire up. A flick of the driver's whip would generally start a team of horses, but it might take half an hour to get up enough steam to drive a steam wagon. This was a minor problem on the railroad, but for personal transport it was very inconvenient.

Leon Serpollet in France came close to success. He built a coal-fired single-seater steam tricycle in 1887. In 1889 he

Leon Serpollet's coal-fired steam tricycle of 1887.

improved it with an "instantaneous" steam generator fueled with paraffin or oil. Serpollet's engine was still "external combustion," but it had shifted to a new fuel, petroleum. It was the "gas buggies" that would make the breakthrough in personal transport, and they would do it with a new kind of engine called the "internal combustion" type.

INTERNAL COMBUSTION AND THE GAS BUGGIES

The internal-combustion engine, the type that provides most of the power for transportation today, was known almost from the beginning of the development of the steam engine. Denis Papin experimented with gunpowder engines, as did Holland's Christian Huygens and also Sadi Carnot, the French scientist who developed the laws of thermodynamics. However, if a steam engine was dangerous, a gunpowder engine was even more so, and not much came of this approach except rocketry, which was not yet ready for personal transportation. Surely personal transportation was not ready for rocketry! Instead, internal-combustion research shifted to explosive gases. Hydrogen was used, and so was "coal gas," a by-product from coal.

As early as 1799 Philip Lebon of France ran an engine on a mixture of coal gas and air, ignited by static electricity. Here was nearly everything needed for a successful gas engine such as powers our vehicles today. But not until Etienne Lenoir's experiments in 1860 with a coal gas engine ignited by a spark from a battery did the internal-combustion engine seriously threaten steam power. Lenoir's engine looked very much like a Watt steam engine, incidentally, with a horizontal cylinder, a flywheel, and even the flyball governor used to regulate engine speed. However, it had a water-cooled jacket and a spark plug not found on steam engines. Coal gas was still a problem fuel because of its expense and the difficulty of handling it safely. Success came only with the liquid fuel, petroleum.

America's first oil well was drilled in 1859, and the new fuel came on strong and fast. In 1864 an Austrian named Siegfried claimed he had powered a small handcart with a petroleum internal-combustion engine. By 1885 Karl Benz was driving around in his personal three-wheeler that somewhat resembled Serpollet's earlier steam car. Fitted with a clutch to disengage the engine from the drive wheels, a carburetor, and a coil-and-battery ignition, the Benz car traveled at about 8 miles an hour. While this was only half the speed of much earlier steam cars, the Benz could be started immediately (if all went well) and was a much lighter and more maneuverable vehicle. By 1893 Benz was manufacturing a four-wheeler automobile with a 3-1/2-horsepower gasoline engine. Hundreds of these were sold and operated in Europe.

Another German inventor, Gottlieb Daimler, developed a high-speed internal-combustion gasoline engine, and in 1886 he drove the first motor bicycle, or motorcycle. A four-wheel

to win its independence. From John Paul Jones' victories on the Great Lakes, naval battles figured in wars right down to World War II. With the coming of nuclear weapons, navies continue to play a part with submarine missile-launchers.

SAILING THE MAN-MADE RIVERS

Canals have long been important for transportation. In the seventh century China put 5½ million people to work on its Grand Canal. After that work was done, the emperor ordered the construction of five hundred large ships, and anyone who refused to work on the project was punished by flogging and neck weights. England built canals totaling four times the length of its navigable rivers and streams.

In America the great canal was the Erie, dreamed of for decades and brought to reality in 1825 by Dewitt Clinton, a smart and hard-working politician who hacked out the ditch that joined the Hudson River with Lake Erie. Immediately the price of shipping freight dropped to 10 percent of earlier costs. Almost as immediately, other states began their own canals, and soon barges and packets were moving up and down the canals, pulled by the current, sails, or steam engines or towed by horses that could pull far more weight in that way then they could over a road.

The Erie Canal took eight years to build—not surprising, since it was 363 miles long. But when it was opened, it in turn opened the midwest. Freight rates plummeted, and passenger travel boomed. By 1840 it was possible to travel 1,100 miles from New York to Cincinnatti almost entirely by water. Soon there were thousands of vessels along the canal and on Lake Erie. No one in those days could foretell the pollution of that great body by waste from the traffic and industry the Erie Canal helped to bring in our time.

Steamboating was the way to travel on rivers like the mighty Mississippi. Thousands of puffing paddlewheelers carried goods and people, and showboats and gambling ships were popular for short trips. The last operating riverboat was

The Suez Canal, designed by Ferdinand de Lesseps, reduced the distance between London and Bombay to 6,442 miles. The voyage around the Cape is more than 11,000 miles.

condemned and removed from the Mississippi only a few years ago, and then with a great fanfare of emotional and legal appeals. But' there was no east-west river in America. The canals carried travelers and merchandise to Chicago, and that was about the end of the line west. A passenger could sail south but no farther toward the new western frontier. Sea voyagers still had to sail for months to reach America's west coast. Canals of a different kind were needed.

In the four years from 1865 to 1869, French engineer Ferdinand de Lesseps built the great Suez Canal, joining the Mediterranean with the Red Sea and thus lopping off thousands of miles of sea travel for many routes. A crude waterway had been dug there thousands of years earlier, but in the intervening centuries the level of lakes fell and the canal went into disrepair. De Lesseps' canal was 107 miles long and nearly 200 feet wide and used no locks. Some fifteen years later, de Lesseps and a group of associates began to carve a sea-level canal across the Isthmus of Panama to eliminate the long sea trip around "the Horn" of South America and thus put the West Coast a month closer to New York. But De Lesseps met more than his match that time, and the attempt failed after he went bankrupt on the new canal. It was up to Theodore Roosevelt, as President of the United States, to pick up the shovel and try again in 1903.

The Suez had taken four years; the Panama Canal took ten. It cost $366 million dollars to build fifty miles of canal with locks to raise and lower the level of the water along the way. Only a miracle of medical science wiped out the dread yellow fever menace that had felled fifty thousand of De Lesseps' workers. But in 1914, when a French ship sailed through the canal in less than ten hours, a new era of sea travel had begun. The canal saved thousands of miles of travel around the entire South American Continent.

The Gallant Clipper Ships

After the war for independence, and as America began the long fight toward the nation we are today, the same shipbuilders who had put together fast and rugged fighting craft turned their art to the great clipper ships. Clipper comes from the Dutch word "klepper," for a high-stepping horse, and the American clippers surely showed their heels to the rest of the marine world.

In 1851 the American ship *Flying Cloud,* built by New England's Donald McKay, sailed from New York to San Francisco in just under ninety days to set a new record on her maiden voyage. Another McKay clipper, *Sovereign of the Seas,* in 1853 logged the greatest distance ever sailed in a single day, 424 nautical miles (equal to almost 485 statute or

The clipper ship *Flying Cloud. Currier & Ives.*

land miles). That was an average speed of 20 miles an hour, using no fuel and producing no pollution.

The clippers carried goods and passengers from Europe to America in less than two weeks, and their captains could still laugh at the challenge of noisy, dirty, and dangerous steamships. In 1853 *Sovereign of the Seas* raced the steamship *Canada* to England. After the first five days it had pulled 325 miles ahead of the steam-powered ship. But change was in the wind, and the days of sailing ships for navies or for commerce were numbered: the wind slackened on the last part of the voyage, and *Canada* reached port two days ahead of the *Sovereign.*

VICTORY FOR STEAM

The days of "wooden ships and iron men" were romantic and exciting, but the iron ships were coming on slowly. Fulton steamed along the Hudson in the *Clermont* in 1807 and wrote an account of his success to the editor of the newspaper *American Citizen:*

> I arrived this afternoon at 4 o'clock, in the steamboat, from Albany. As the success of my experiment gives me great hope that such boats may be rendered of much importance to my country, to prevent erroneous opinions, and give some satisfaction to the friends of useful improvements, you will have the goodness to publish the following statement of facts: . . .

His facts were indeed impressive—trips of 110 miles and 150 miles on consecutive days. However, success was not instantaneous, and it was twelve more years before the steamship *Savannah* sailed across the Atlantic. Even then there were no passengers aboard the craft, or even a cargo, for no passengers or shippers were foolhardy enough yet to trust such a dangerous, smoky ship. She had fuel enough for only eighty hours of the voyage, anyhow, so she actually steamed a little more than three days of the several weeks. Ironically, the *Savannah* was later converted by her owners into a sailing ship, and that was the end of steam on the ocean for a decade. So discouraging were the prospects that Dionysus Lardner, an English nautical authority, wrote that there was about as much hope of sailing a steamship across the Atlantic as there was of traveling to the moon.

In 1833, however, the *Royal William* steamed clear across the Atlantic in twenty-three days, and the great Cunard Steamship Lines was born. In England, a dynamic young man named Isambard Kingdom Brunel, who was building a railroad line called the Great Western, decided he would like it to reach all the way to New York instead of stopping when it reached Bristol from London. So he built the huge *Great*

Western steamship and sailed it to New York in 1837. When the *Great Western* made the trip in just fifteen days, the era of steamships across the ocean had begun.

Brunel followed up the *Great Western* with a much larger *Great Eastern*. This sea giant was built at a cost of more than $5 million and was a total failure financially, but it started marine designers in the direction of the huge ocean liners that for more than half a century would rule the seas.

When England gave Samuel Cunard a mail contract for his steamboats he was soon crossing the Atlantic on schedules of little over ten days, no matter what the wind. The hot competition that followed was not just American pride but hardheaded business. Speed was important for mail and for business travel, but it made a great difference to ordinary passengers too. If a competing line offered the trip in a day less, it would get the traffic. A peaceful sea war began between America and England, with France, Germany, and others getting into the battle for good measure. At stake was the coveted and symbolic "Blue Riband" or Blue Ribbon, and a generation of ocean liners vied for the speed record, with the trophy going back and forth through the years.

Great advances were required between the *Great Western*'s pioneering two-week trip and regular crossings of less than four days. Coal-burning steam engines gave way to Diesel, and then turbines came to be the accepted engines. England's Charles Parsons ushered in that new engine in 1894 by racing past a great flotilla of conventional craft in his *Turbinia* at the fantastic speed of thirty-five knots.

So important was maritime transportation that great insurance firms developed to insure cargoes. Among them was the historic "Lloyds of London," still doing business throughout the world. Lloyds first used telescopes and semaphore signals to speed news of ships. But Italian inventor Marconi's wireless made it possible to talk instantaneously to vessels a hundred, even a thousand, miles away. Gyro-stabilizers, radio, and better navigation techniques were also developed. Ships pursued the polar explorations begun by the earlier sailing vessels.

There were tragedies, of course, just as there were tragedies on the railroads spreading across continents. Ships hit rocks, icebergs, and each other, to sink and take helpless victims with them to the bottom. Ships exploded and burned. The mighty *Titanic*, believed to be unsinkable, set a terrible record of almost 1,600 lives lost when she rammed an iceberg. The *Lusitania* was a victim of torpedoes in World War I. The navies had kept pace with commercial ships, and fast surface vessels were joined by the submarine, which Robert Fulton had demonstrated years earlier.

Brunel's *Great Western* was the first winner of the Blue Ribbon. Early in the twentieth century France's *Mauretania* set a record of four days, ten hours and forty-one minutes, a mark not broken for nearly twenty-five years. Eventually Germany's *Bremen* did the trick, followed by the Italian liner *Rex*, the French *Normandie*, and then Britain's majestic *Queen Mary*, which made it in three days, twenty hours, and forty-two minutes. In 1952 the *United States* captured the Blue Ribbon with a time of three days, ten hours, and forty minutes. No ship has beaten that remarkable speed.

THE WANING OF SEA POWER

Like the railroads, ships did yeoman service in World War II, in commercial traffic as well as in the navies. After the war there was a brief, wonderful period for trans-Atlantic liners. They offered marvelous service—excellent food, great safety, and speedy travel across the big pond. But competition appeared overhead. The feeble little airplanes had grown wings large enough and motors strong enough to carry them across 2,500 miles of open water. Lindbergh had proved it could be done in 1927. By the 1950s airliners were doing it with full loads of passengers. No longer did motor ships rule the sea.

CHAPTER
6

The Great Iron Horse

America's first railroad, the famous Baltimore & Ohio, used cars drawn by horses. On January 1, 1830, one horse pulled a B. & O. railroad car loaded with twenty-four passengers at a speed of 15 miles an hour. That was a remarkable job for a one-horsepower engine. Today we often call on hundreds of horsepower to carry just one person.

Even loaded with eighty passengers, the one-horse railroad made a speed of eight miles an hour. It was a great financial success, and the short line (only thirteen miles long, from Baltimore, Maryland, to Ellicott's Mills) grossed a thousand dollars a week in its first month of operation.

The horse-car could not long prevail, however. Although the pioneering steam locomotive, *Tom Thumb*, was beaten by a horse-drawn train in a race, it later made a speed of 18 miles an hour. As somebody pointed out, *Tom Thumb* did not get nearly as tired as the horse did.

Soon a bigger and better locomotive was pulling five cars loaded with 150 people at 15 miles an hour. The great event was reported in the Washington *Daily Intelligencer* on September 2, 1830:

> The first Railroad car, propelled by steam, proceeded the whole distance from Baltimore to Ellicott's Mills on Saturday last, . . . We congratulate our fellow-citizens on the conclusive proof which removed forever all doubt on this subject, and establishes the fact that steam power may be used on our road with as much facility and effect as that of horses, at a very reduced expense.

The Tom Thumb built by Peter Cooper, was a small engine of about one horsepower mounted on a small car frame and geared to an axle. *Association of American Railroads.*

A replica of the pioneer horse car used on the Baltimore & Ohio Railroad in 1829. In 1830 the horse car won a race with the Tom Thumb. *Association of American Railroads.*

The first trains were ridden for entertainment, as were the "omnibuses" in Europe. Many critics said they would soon fade away as all fads did, but the railroad was no freak sport. Almost immediately the new transportation system doubled and tripled business. The initial 20-passengers-a-day volume on the B. & O. grew quickly to 120. Train travel was not just a service to shippers and businessmen but a business in its own right and a powerful force in the growth of the country.

The year 1830 was a magic one for railroads in America. Charleston business men built the South Carolina Railroad, and before the year's end there was regular rail service offering speeds of more than 20 miles an hour. New Orleans, the home port of hundreds of paddlewheel steamers, had a railroad as well; so did Kentucky and New England.

There were problems, to be sure. The South Carolina's locomotive *Best Friend of Charleston* exploded when the engineer sat on the safety valve to silence its annoying whistle! But engineers were learning, and better equipment was being built. The horse's career on the railroad was finished and so were the brave but impractical "sailing cars" that were tried out. A few wind wagons were built in later years, and they had some great adventures on the western prairies, but it was steam that drove the thundering iron horse clear across the country to the Pacific Ocean.

Early trains were crude steam engines hauling several stagecoaches fitted with flanged iron wheels. But soon the traditional boxlike railroad car evolved. Cars were joined together with lengths of chain, and they jerked wildly when starting and crashed into each other on stopping before better coupling devices were invented. Screens were later put on smokestacks to stop the worst of the blazing embers from setting passengers afire.

The first rails were of wood. Later, the wood was covered with thin straps of iron, but that still made a flimsy, shortlived track. When American railroad builder Robert Stevens sailed to England to order strap-iron rails for his new Camden and

Amboy Railroad, he found a block of wood and began to whittle out a design for something more durable. His model for the T-shaped iron rail soon became standard. Before long, sturdy iron rails were an inseparable part of the American countryside, rolled over by the nation's trains and walked upon by most of the nation's youth. It took longer to standardize the "gauge," or width between the iron rails.

Even the ancient cart tracks in Malta had a standard width, but in the beginning of American railroading each company had a measurement of its own. The Baltimore & Ohio used a track width of four feet, eight and a half inches, copying English locomotive builders. They, in turn, had simply adopted the width of English horse-drawn carts. Some railway lines had tracks as narrow as three feet, four inches. Erie Railroad tracks were six feet apart. Congress eventually passed legislation for transcontinental lines making four feet, eight and a half inches the national standard, but we have many smaller "narrow-gauge" railroads still in operation. Most of them are short, scenic routes that once served logging or other special uses.

TRACKS TO EVERYWHERE

In 1830 there were only about twenty-five miles of railroad track in the United States. By 1837 there were nearly 1,500. Rail travel was beginning to challenge the extensive canal systems that were being completed, including De Witt Clinton's great Erie Canal. Then overinvestment in railroads and canals, combined with land speculation, caused the "panic of 1837," which abruptly stopped the wildfire growth of railroading.

Critics declared that the railroad bubble had burst for good, but by 1840 the track length had doubled again to almost three thousand miles, and it was possible to ride on trains all the way from Maine to the Carolinas. Particularly in regions where there were few canals, the railroad flourished. Tracks were being laid even in Pennsylvania's rugged mountains.

Farther west, Michigan and Ohio were building furiously. In 1850 there were 9,000 miles of track; by 1860, more than 30,000 miles. Twenty years before, railroads had just about matched the canals in length, but by that time the railroads had increased about tenfold while canals had extended only a few hundred miles. It was obvious who had won the battle.

Using Samuel Morse's new telegraph, railroads dispatched their trains by wire, speeding and improving service. The U.S. government and also the states began to help railroad builders with loans and even with outright grants of land along proposed rail lines. The greatest advance in railroading came with the first transcontinental line, the Union Pacific, a development made inevitable by the discovery of gold in California and the consequent growth of that state.

As a newly admitted state in 1850, California had a population of 100,000. Compared with its present 20,000,000, this is sparse indeed, but in those early times 100,000 was a lot of people and the population was growing rapidly. Yet the new land was virtually isolated from the east by thousands of miles of rough country. Many people preferred the tedious ship voyage around the Horn to the rough and dangerous wagon or stagecoach journey.

DRIVING THE GOLDEN SPIKE

California had a few short railroad lines in the 1850s, but they did little good for transcontinental transportation. In 1854 a young engineer named Theodore Judah went to California and became involved in railroading. By 1859 he was convinced that he could build a track through the forbidding Sierra Nevada Mountains. He interested some California backers who were able to get help from the federal government, and in 1861 the Central Pacific Railroad was chartered. In 1862, the Union Pacific obtained much the same sort of charter and financial help. Work on the transcontinental track started from east to west, and from west to east, in the closing days of the Civil War.

Building the first cross-country railroad was a costly and difficult process, slowed by the Civil War and its aftermath; by a labor shortage, which was solved only by importing Chinese coolies; and by hostile Indians who destroyed equipment and killed the railroaders. The work went on, nevertheless, aided by loans ranging from $16,000 to $48,000 per mile of track. Critics have pointed out that much money found its way into the pockets of dishonest men, and surely there were abuses of the public trust. Greedy for the per-mile guarantees, the two companies continued to build parallel tracks after they had met. Congress had to step in and designate Promontory, Utah, as the official juncture of the two tracks.

On May 10, 1869, the official completion ceremony took place. Central Pacific had laid track east from Sacramento, a distance of 689 miles. Union Pacific had built 1,086 miles west from Omaha, Nebraska. It is generally recalled that a golden spike was driven to commemorate the event, but there was more ceremony than that. The last cross tie was of laurel wood brought from California. A pure California gold spike was hammered into it, but there was also one of Nevada silver, and another from Arizona containing gold, silver, and iron. President Leland Stanford, of the Central Pacific, and Thomas Durant, Vice President of Union Pacific, fired off the following telegram:

> To His Excellency, General U.S. Grant, President of the United States: We have the honor to report the last rail laid, the last spike driven. The Pacific Railroad is finished.

It was a great day for railroading, for transportation, and for the country as a whole. By 1870, just forty years from the time *Tom Thumb* was beaten by the horse on a 13-mile run, America could boast of 53,000 miles of railroad track, all of it used by steam locomotives. Even that tremendous growth was only a hint of what was coming. Each mile of track, each

On May 10, 1869, the American continent was spanned by the first chain of railroads as the Union Pacific and Central Pacific (now the Southern Pacific) were joined in Promontory, Utah. *Union Pacific Railroad.*

new locomotive and string of cars, instead of satisfying the needs of travelers and business, seemed to demand even more miles. By 1890 there were 165,000 miles of railroads. Most of the new lines were in the developing west, hauling cattle from Texas and Wyoming, wheat and other crops from new farming states like the Dakotas, and minerals from the Rocky Mountain country. It was not the six-gun but the railroad that really won the West.

MAKING TRAINS SAFER

Along with progress, however, the railroads often brought tragedy. The first recorded fatality on a railroad occurred September 15, 1830, on the Liverpool and Manchester line in England. The victim, run over by Stephenson's *Rocket*, was a friend of the Duke of Wellington. Such calamities were repeated all too often in America. There were catastrophic boiler explosions and fires. Train wrecks were caused by faulty track, crumpling bridges, and falling rocks. Sometimes two trains smashed head on, and sometimes one ran into another from behind. Indians and train-robbers plagued the railroads and their rich cargo of goods and people. Passengers and trainmen were often injured and sometimes killed in accidents. Engineers and firemen were particularly in danger of being scalded to death or crushed in their locomotives. Brakemen were often mangled trying to couple cars with the crude mechanisms then used.

From 1870 to 1890 an average of twenty-five railroad bridges collapsed every year. One that fell in Ohio in 1877 killed ninety people, and the chief engineer of the railroad line involved committed suicide. Such casualties were accepted as inevitable, though regrettable, results of the great need to build railroads to serve the growing, booming United States. Public reaction was somewhat like the shrugging acceptance of the shady financial dealings that were overlooked to get the railroads built. Only in the 1870s was there finally enough time to take a breathing spell and a hard look at the shortcomings of the railroads.

George Westinghouse was only twenty-three years old when he set up his company in 1869 to build air brakes for the railroads. It took him about twenty years to perfect his system, but by then railroads had become far safer, and it was possible to stop a train in a fraction of the distance it once took. The "Janney coupler" was a similar improvement over manual methods of hooking one car to another, a dangerous task that often cost the hands, arms, or lives of brakemen. In 1893 Congress passed a law that all railroad cars in interstate commerce must use the safe new coupler, and by 1905 all trains were so equipped. Trains had often killed people at unguarded crossings. Westinghouse and others developed safety equipment of many types, and gradually the accident toll was cut.

SHRINKING A NATION

Railroads played a vital part in the great drama of growth in our country. The books, movies, and songs that have immortalized the railroads have exaggerated very little. At its peak, railroad trackage had increased ten thousand times from the modest twenty-five miles in 1830 to ten times the circumference of the world. Railroads were everywhere, and their effect on society was revolutionary. After they came, life could never again be the same, much as traditionalists might want to cling to the past. One apparent effect was a considerable shrinkage of the country's physical size.

"Death Valley Scotty," the legendary gold prospector of California, lived through an era when it took a month of hard travel to get from California back East. But in 1905 Scotty chartered a Santa Fe train for a record-breaking run from Los Angeles to Chicago in less than forty-five hours. Not until 1934 was that mark beaten by Union Pacific with its new "streamliner," which made the same run in less than thirty-nine hours and traveled all the way to New York in less than fifty-seven hours.

Generally, travelers had hesitated to make journeys farther than they could travel in a single day. In stagecoach times, a trip of fifty miles was about the limit of a day's travel. However, in spite of London scientists who warned that trains could never go faster than thirty miles an hour without suffocating their passengers, and Munich doctors who feared that such speed would cause a new mental illness termed *delerium furiosum*, the railroad made it possible for the traveler to go fifty miles in an hour, and a thousand miles in a day. Railroads thus extended the range of travel twenty-fold in less than a century, shrinking our nation to a convenient size for anyone with the price of a railroad ticket.

TROUBLE ON THE TRACKS

For a long time the railroads had it all their own way. They met and beat the competition of stagecoaches, steamships, and canal boats, and they did it gloriously. But shortly after 1900 two new competitors began to challenge the great iron horse. While Henry Ford was tinkering with his first "Tin Lizzie," two Ohio bicycle mechanics named Wilbur and Orville Wright were putting together an even more revolutionary form of transportation, the first airplane. Since that time population, travel, and shipping in the United States have doubled, but the railroad's business has not kept up with the increase. Instead it has lost ground, as indicated in the fact that track length has shrunk to only 220,000 miles from its peak of 250,000 in the great golden age of railroads.

In the 1930s the railroads tried valiantly to meet the new challenge on the highways and airways with a generation of "Zephyrs," "Chiefs" and other streamlined trains. The old, smoky coal-burners were replaced by diesel-electrics. Luxurious passenger cars replaced the old Civil War boxes that had served on some lines until the Depression and even through World War II. Food service was improved, music was provided, and such luxuries as "vista domes" offered spectacular scenic views. Air conditioning and other improvements were made. Nevertheless, the railroads steadily lost ground.

During World War II it seemed that the dying railroads might rise like Phoenix birds from their own ashes. The tremendous demands of the military effort, plus a shortage of gasoline for private vehicles, challenged the railroads with some of the most productive years of their century-old life. Out of retirement came ancient passenger cars, some with antique lanterns still swinging on the walls and the same impossible-to-move windows jamming to roast passengers in hot weather and freeze them in cold. But the same war triggered the huge federal "Defense Highway" system that accelerated the post-war rush to the open road in one's own automobile. While cars, trucks, and buses profited, the railroads were hurt all the more.

In many instances, whole systems that had for years made a great contribution to transportation were eliminated, and their rights of way were disposed of for other purposes. The Pacific Electric commuter service in and around Los Angeles was an example. Railroading is a business, and few lines can afford to stay on if they are losing money.

The wrack and ruin of New England's once great commuter lines and the financial disasters of the famed Penn Central are other examples of the fall of the once ruling giant of transportation. Who is to blame? The answers are varied and controversial. Much of the fault must lie with a business grown complacent during decades with little or no competition. When competition came, it was difficult to change the established patterns of century-old empires.

There were other reasons. Early in their growth the railroads had to turn to government for help, and with that help came regulation and control. Government agencies have not always acted in the best interests of the railroads, shippers, or even the traveling public. Railroads have often been forced to continue unprofitable routes. Sometimes they have been denied the right to cut prices and to start new runs that would be profitable and contribute to the public good as well. Labor too has been a problem, for regulations and wage structures established half a century ago still prevail. The railroad industry charges that "feather-bedding," the practice by unions of maintaining the jobs of employees no longer needed, saddles them with more losses.

Profitable mail contracts dwindled as the airlines began to carry an increasing share of the load. Why send mail by train when planes could get it there in a fraction of the time? Even in the freight business the airlines cut into railroad's share, and trucks took a huge slice of the pie.

The ills of the railroads are much like the ancient riddle of the chicken and the egg. Did the railroads lose out because of their own poor service, or did poor service come after competition caused them to fail? The same government that had once helped fledgling railroads get moving now gave major assistance to highways and airlines. Passengers who earlier had happily deserted stagecoaches and steamboats for trains now left the trains to line up at bus depots and air terminals. But there was an even greater threat to railroad travel from "personal transport." Long ago John Ruskin voiced a complaint that many travelers must have felt: "Railway traveling is not traveling at all; it is merely being sent to a place, and very little different from becoming a parcel."

Weary of being just parcels "sent to a place" people could now set out in their own automobiles and make the trip faster and often more pleasantly. "Two cars in every garage" came close to reality, and it was foolish not to use them.

THE SUPERTRAINS FIGHT BACK

Halfway around the world, however, Japan showed what could be done by trains. Along historic Tokkaido Road, which has for centuries linked the eastern and western parts of the island, Japan National Railways built a high-speed track between the great cities of Tokyo and Osaka. Carefully engineered through the scenic countryside and much of it on elevated roadbed, the track was for a new breed of supertrains, put into operation during the 1964 Olympic Games.

In olden times a traveler along the Tokkaido Road could make the long journey in about two weeks on foot, and that was the way most traveling was done then. In 1872 Japan built its first railroad. By 1964 it was possible to travel by train from Tokyo to Osaka in six hours and forty minutes, and few dreamed of going faster than that. But the "Bullet Express" did, clipping along the 320 miles of perfect track as fast as 130 miles an hour to make the complete trip in just three hours and ten minutes. The long-dreamed-of "100-mile-an hour railroad" had arrived, at a cost of $1.5 billion.

Japan uses railroads far more than any other nation. Drawing from a population of 100 million, its trains carry something like 10 billion passengers a year. On the average, every citizen in Japan rides the train a hundred times a year! Most of the country's commuting is done by rail instead of highway as in the United States. So crushing is the load that Japanese railroads employ "pushers" to pack commuters into the crowded trains. They do their job so well that during rush hour the trains carry two and a half times as many passengers as there are seats. Once crammed inside, however, the traveler is assured a fast trip that gets him where he is going on schedule, something that cannot always be said for commuter trains in our country.

Belatedly it dawned on planners of our nation's transportation effort that the train still has a place in the total system; that trains can run when airplanes are grounded by weather, and that it is possible even in good weather to beat plane schedules on a downtown-to-downtown basis with faster trains. In the east, "Metroliners" and "Turbo-trains" have demonstrated what they could do and can pack their cars with passengers in spite of higher fares.

The Turbo-Train, built by Sikorsky, an aircraft manufacturer, uses aircraft turbine engines for efficiency, cleanliness, speed, quiet operation and economy. On a special section of track along the regular run, the Turbo-Train has exceeded 170 miles an hour, although it averages only 75 miles an hour from Boston to New York. Even this is more than 20 miles an hour faster than conventional train schedules. Canada's Canadian National line adopted Turbo-Trains to reduce its 335-mile run between Montreal to Toronto from five hours to four.

WHO WILL SAVE THE RAILROADS?

Desperate measures have been taken by the railroads, and some clever new techniques are working to rescue them from failure. There are "piggyback" freight operations in which truck trailers are loaded aboard freight trains for long hauls; freight cars perform a similar trick on "fishyback" barges and ships. Scenic rail trips have been promoted in many areas from New England to Colorado and Arizona. Special trains take skiers and other sports enthusiasts to recreation spots. A few new commuter trains offer modest fares, good food, and other diversions to commuters weary of the freeway.

In spite of their problems, the railroads are still a major business, with almost 600,000 employees and a gross income of $12 billion in 1970. They carry more than 40 percent of the freight between cities, including two thirds of the coal, automobiles, lumber, iron and steel, and household appliances. Railroading is a profitable career. A railroad engineer can make from $25,000 to $30,000 a year, and there are many other positions available to young people looking for work.

Nevertheless, the retreat has continued. More and more railroads have gone bankrupt and been forced to sell off the huge business holdings they acquired over the years. Some railroad men have committed suicide in despair. Recently the government has stepped in with its "Amtrak" operation in a desperate attempt to "save the railroads," an effort many critics say is doomed to fail. Ironically, one of Amtrak's first moves was to drop many passenger lines, in an attempt to save the more important runs. That move did not set very well with those deprived of even the little service they formerly had.

Some of the most pessimistic voices are those of railroad executives themselves. The head of one large railroad has said that Amtrak can do no more than "preside over an orderly shrinkage of rail passenger service." On the other hand, Amtrak's director stated in 1972 that his organization was operating thirty trains more than when it took over in 1970, and that in five years passenger traffic would double or triple. The future of the great iron horse is very obviously in doubt. The questions of whether the railroads are worth saving, if they can be saved, who will do it, and how, have yet to be answered. We will return to this problem in Chapter 9.

CHAPTER
7

Automobiles:
"Personal Transport"

When we are caught on the freeway during rush hour, the thought comes naturally that the automobile is one of our worst inventions and it would be great to return to the good old days before it took over the roads. Perhaps the only people who have not dreamed such dreams are those fortunate enough never to drive in heavy traffic—or those who have more carefully thought through the situation. For it is important to realize that a nation does not willingly give up something good and replace it with something bad. Let's look realistically at the world before the coming of personal transportation in the form of the automobile.

Traffic jams are nothing new; they date back to early London, ancient Rome, and probably the great cities at the dawn of civilization. Rome, ruled by dictators for most of its history, surely had strict laws that were rigidly enforced. Yet that city suffered from congestion, as might be expected of a city to which all roads led! London, particularly in later years when personal freedoms were growing, was an even more densely crowded city, and old woodcuts may make us question how good the "good old days" really were.

The streets of London were jammed with people. People afoot, and people riding animals. People aboard wagons and coaches and omnibuses. People jostling, pushing, and shoving. People choked by London's perpetual smoke. There was little or no control of traffic, and vehicles proceeded at a snail's pace. There was noise pollution too. And there was something else, "nose pollution" few of us today could stand. Yet Londoners probably seldom bothered to complain, for there was little that could be done about it, short of eliminating horses and other animals as motive power for vehicles. In spite of the bad smell and the hazardous walking conditions, wagons and carriages were better than walking everywhere on one's own feet and carrying everything on one's own back.

As America's cities grew, they too inherited that unfortunate aspect of big-city life. Americans learned the frustrations of trying to urge a balky horse or mule to negotiate a muddy, rutted road, and occasionally the terror of fleeing a runaway team. Animals also had to be sheltered, fed, and cared for. It was not a simple matter of turning a crank to get them moving. Animals had temperament, perhaps even more than that of the first automobiles. As early as Greek times, a writer suggested that the only way to keep a mule in good working order was to ply him with great quantities of wine! Actually, the coming of the automobile was hailed as a great blessing when it made its sputtering appearance on city streets at the turn of the century.

COMING OF THE MOTOR AGE

In 1895 a new magazine appeared in America. It was called *Horseless Age,* a title that indicated how horse-oriented our people were at that time. They could only think negatively from the horse, and the magazine *Motor Age* did not appear for some time. *Horseless Age* promised readers that not only was the automobile coming but an entirely new civilization would roll into town with it. It was a very accurate prediction, for the automobile and other powered vehicles have made our lives far different than they were before. It is true that in recent years the automobile has become a safety hazard, a great congester of highways and polluter of air as well as a troublesome noisemaker. But great and valid hopes were raised for it in those early days.

Reminding its readers of the obvious—the noise of wagon wheels on cobblestones, balky animals, and manure in the streets—*Horseless Age* pointed out that "The nuisance will not be wholly abated until the great beasts whose refuse litters the streets and fouls the atmosphere in our populous centers are banished from the cities."

The new magazines were advertising automobiles, of course, and their editors were not above exaggeration if it suited their purposes. However, there was much truth in what they said. Those who fought the coming of the automobile were accused of having "motorphobia," just as earlier "Luddites" in England had fought the introduction of weaving machines in the factories.

In 1899 *Scientific American* agreed with *Horseless Age* and strongly urged the acceptance of the automobile for a number of reasons, all of them hard to argue against three-quarters of a century ago:

> The improvement in city conditions by the general adoption of the motor car can hardly be overestimated. Streets clean, dustless and odorless, with light rubber-tired vehicles moving swiftly and noiseless over their smooth expanse, would eliminate a greater part of the nervousness, distraction, and strain of modern metropolitan life.

It may come as a shock today to realize that before the turn of the century we had any "modern metropolitan life," and that it was plagued by nervousness, strain, and distraction. As automobiles began to chug about the streets, the praise for them grew in spite of all the horses they scared with their raucous backfiring. One commentator, writing in the *Independent* in 1904, described life in the coming motor age:

Imagine a healthier race of workingmen, toiling in cheerful and sanitary factories . . . who, in the late afternoon, glide away in their own comfortable vehicles to their little farms or homes in the country or by the sea twenty or thirty miles distant! They will be healthier, happier, more intelligent and self-respecting citizens because of the chance to live among the meadows and flowers of the country instead of in crowded city streets.

It is difficult for most of us today to appreciate what living in the city was and still is for some unfortunate "inner city" dwellers. *Munsey's Magazine* published an article in which its editor hailed the automobile as wonderful therapy for suffering mankind:

It is the greatest health-giving invention of a thousand years. The cubic feet of fresh air that are literally forced into one while automobiling rehabilitate worn-out nerves and drive out worry, insomnia, and indigestion. It will renew the life and youth of the overworked man or woman, and will make the thin fat and the fat thin—but I forbear.

Today such claims would be immediately investigated by a disciple of Ralph Nader; surely Mr. Munsey exaggerated the automobile's virtues and was blind to its vices. Today the air forced into us on a crowded freeway may contain dangerous amounts of pollutants from the automobile. It is a sad fact that suicides often turn to the automobile, running a hose from its carbon-monoxide-producing exhaust pipe into the car. And yet it is almost impossible to imagine a world suddenly without the automobile. As *Horseless Age* and many other magazines pointed out, the automobile revolutionized human life, and not all of that revolution was bad.

In olden times a fifty-mile journey was an event that took time, money, and often courage. Today we often get into a car and travel 500 miles or more between morning and night.

We can ride in air-conditioned comfort of a kind that stage-coach passengers could not have imagined in their most optimistic dreams. Automobiles make it possible for people to commute to jobs fifty miles away, and to live on "the little farm, or by the sea," as *Independent* magazine promised seventy years ago. The average automobile in America travels about 12,000 miles a year, and many families drive two or more cars. Our forefathers might not travel that distance in a lifetime; many never got farther from home all their lives than we can in an hour.

One entry in the great Paris-to-Bordeaux automobile race of 1895 was equipped with a kitchen and a toilet. Several decades ago, industry belatedly picked up that revolution in living by making the automobile trailer possible. Now the automobile itself has become the mobile home, and a new generation of nomads are taking to the roads like the gypsies of an earlier day.

It is only one example of the great flexibility made possible by the automobile. An admirer wrote in 1903: "One lives three times as much in the same span of years," and in 1909 *Harper's Weekly* pointed out that the automobile gave "the feeling of independence—the freedom from timetables, from fixed and inflexible routes, from the proximity of other human beings than one's own chosen companions; the ability to go where and when one wills, to linger and stop where the country is beautiful and the way pleasant . . ." These glowing predictions were true at the time, and the automobile has accomplished so much of what was promised that we must think carefully before giving it up.

THE TROUBLE WITH AUTOMOBILES

Not all predictions were correct, of course. For instance, one writer felt that by making life on the farm so pleasant, the automobile would "keep 'em down on the farm," and might even cause a shift away from the city. That has not happened. Instead, the process of urbanization has increased, and largely because of the automobile. Perhaps the greatest error the early glowing tributes and predictions made was not to foresee the tremendous increase in population and in number of automobiles. Ironically, the automobile's greatest problem is its success. No one has forced us to produce automobiles in such numbers. They obviously must offer something in return for costs that continually rise, fuel and maintenance, taxes, and the host of other expenses connected with owning and operating a motor vehicle.

In self defense we make jokes about the increase in car population. "Take two; they're small," refers to the influx of "import" cars that are now coming out of Detroit's factories too. "Everyone has two cars now and drives both of them at once," is a common complaint. A tongue-in-cheek prediction claims that since fifty years ago there were an average of 2.2 people in each automobile on the road, and twenty years ago only 1.2 people, in ten years there will be only a half of a person in each car! The element of truth in all these comments is that the vehicle population now challenges that of humans. At one time we had millions of horses and mules pulling our wagons and carriages. Today we have a hundred million motor vehicles.

Actually, it is a miracle that traffic problems are not even worse. A recent science-fiction story might easily come true: On one sad day for motorists, everyone decided to go to the same place at the same time, with the result that a monumental traffic jam ensued. After that, the only solution was to assign people different days of the week for driving, so there would be room on the highways. In our own era, when Zero Population Growth is a catchy slogan, there seems to be no similar effort to check the growth of our motorized population. Few people see any harm in having three cars, a pickup truck, a dune buggy, a mobile home, two motorbikes, and a snowmobile in one household.

At some point between 1900 and the present, highway travel probably was ideal, with just the right number of vehicles and cubic feet of fresh air per square yards of pavement. Today that optimum point has long been passed. Today's freeway builders have been accused of "pouring more concrete than Pharaoh ever dreamed of," and we have more than 3 ½ million miles of streets and highways; yet all the millions of vehicles on the road make this outpouring not enough and many of those miles are lined bumper-to-bumper. Some pessimists say that the only solution is to pour cement over the whole colossal traffic tie-up and start all over with some other transportation idea. The trouble is that not many sensible ideas are brought forth to take the place of the automobile and its growing stranglehold on modern civilization.

POLLUTION

Society was sold on the automobile partly because it promised to eliminate the pollution of horses and other beasts of burden. Now the noise of engines, screaming tires and brakes, horns, and sirens far exceeds the old clatter of wheels on cobblestones. More unfortunately yet, the wastes from motor vehicles—carbon monoxide, nitrogen, and hydrocarbons, while not as disgusting as animal wastes, are potentially more deadly. In earlier times there was a "horse brigade" that went around sweeping up after horses. Sweeping up the atmosphere after automobiles is a much more difficult task and has not yet been successfully achieved.

Slowly the atmosphere grows dirtier in and around big cities—and even far out in the wilds, many miles from big cities. Airliners grope their way to landings through brownish stains that blot out airports even in broad daylight. On the ground, motorists have a twofold visibility problem: the air is thick with smoke, and their eyes water from the acrid chemicals contained in that smoke. In some cities traffic policemen must wear oxygen masks in self-defense. Each year millions of tons of garbage are spewed into the atmosphere. Air pollution has become a major problem around the world and much of the blame must fall on automobiles. Pollution is being pumped from exhaust pipes, engines, tires, and even brake drums, and unconcerned drivers and passengers are adding their own solid waste litter to the roads.

THE GREAT FUEL SHORTAGE

Another problem that is not as obvious as fatalities, crowding, and pollution is the shortage of fuel, which increasingly troubles government officials and industrialists concerned with that vital area of supply and demand. Horses ate grain and other expendable foods, but the sun grows more oats, barley, and hay each year. The early steam engines could run on wood, but coal soon took over, and then oil and gasoline became standard. They still are, and there is only so much of these "fossil fuels," for nature takes millions of years to make them. The United States, the greatest consumer, must import a good share of its fuels. We are at such a crucial point of shortage that gasoline rationing presently threatens Los Angeles and other urban areas. What an excellent way to end traffic congestion, air pollution, and fatalities all at once! Unfortunately it would end a lot of other things as well— things like commuting to a job, carrying freight, and taking pleasure trips.

There is growing interest in power plants other than the conventional internal-combustion engine. Manufacturers are attempting to produce steam engines for autos and buses. While it is claimed by some that silent, clean and maintenance-free electric cars can't work, the fact is that they did work as personal vehicles more than seventy years ago, and performed as taxis, delivery vans, and even race cars exceeding 65 miles an hour. Critics complain that electrics are too slow, too limited in range, or too productive of ozone, which may be a bigger polluter than the noxious gases from the gasoline engine. With more validity, they correctly point out that electricity does not grow on trees any more than oil or gasoline. It still must be produced mostly by mechanical engines powered by fossil fuels.

The world's first sun-driven automobile is powered by a huge panel of more than 10,000 individual silicon solar cells mounted on the roof. Car used is a renovated 1912 electric Baker. *International Rectifier Corp.*

The rotary gasoline engine is proving successful and may solve some automotive problems. The Stirling-cycle hot-air engine is another "external-combustion" engine, somewhat like the steam engine, and a few test vehicles are powered by this type. Hailed as even more promising are "hybrid" systems in which fuel cells produce electricity for motive power. Fuel cells produce no harmful exhaust, and some produce only fresh water as waste. They also eliminate the need for the frequent and time-consuming recharging of batteries.

KILLERS ON THE HIGHWAY

We are a nation addicted to a habit we have just found out is killing us, yet we cannot rid ourselves of that habit. It is no exaggeration to say that automobiles are killing us, of course. In 1972 more than 57,000 people died on our streets and highways as a result of accidents. Millions more were injured, some of them crippled for the rest of their lives. The automobile has the highest fatality rate of any major transportation method. It is several times more dangerous than aircraft and tens of times more dangerous than rail travel.

It is doubtful that anyone ever suffocated from the tremendous speed of an automobile, or that *delirium furiosum* took a heavy toll of lives, as some agitated experts predicted. But the automobile by its nature has inherent dangers. In its early days there were many broken arms from cranking cars, and it was reported that one man broke his jaw while performing that dangerous task and later died of his injuries. But the worst was yet to come.

In 1895, when there were still only two automobiles in the entire state of Ohio, two of them nevertheless managed to collide head-on in the mainstreet of a town. One driver died as a result of his injuries. Four years later, an unfortunate man named Henry Bliss became the first pedestrian victim. He was killed by an automobile in New York City as he alighted from a horse-drawn streetcar.

Soon there had to be crosswalks and stoplights and traffic policemen. Nevertheless, the two million auto fatalities dating back from the U.S. withdrawal from Vietnam in 1973 nearly doubled *all the deaths occurring in all our wars* up to that time—not just from 1895, but from the birth of our country in 1776.

We have spoken of the freedom the automobile affords. Tragically, that includes the freedom to drive in an intoxicated condition. Although it is clear that at least half the fatalities on the highways are caused by drunk drivers, society at large either does not care or is powerless to reduce the toll.

A passenger car rams a specially designed wall in a safety test. *Dynamic Science.*

Buses, trains, and planes have far fewer drunks at the controls and thus, if only for this reason, are not as deadly killers as automobiles. Public transportation is better maintained, too, for automobile drivers resist laws that require the inspection and proper maintenance of their vehicles. Thus thousands of lost lives are part of the price we pay for our traditional "freedom of the open road."

Occasionally a car enthusiast adds a light tank, bought from war surplus, to his stable of vehicles, jokingly remarking that he feels safer driving with such protection. Perhaps there is more truth than humor in such a statement. One approach to auto safety is to surround the driver and passengers in a cocoon of steel so that they can ram, or be rammed by, just about anything and survive. More moderate approaches include seat belts and shoulder harnesses, which are fairly standard equipment, although many riders fail to buckle up for safety. Air bags are being experimented with, and so are more-effective bumpers, safety glass, and other equipment.

THE MACHINE AGAINST MAN?

At about the beginning of this century, as automobiles began to invade even the remoteness of the western states, the Nebraska Legislature wrote the following humorous vehicle code into its law books:

> On approaching a corner where he cannot command a view of the road ahead, the automobilist must stop not less than 100 yards from the turn, toot his horn, ring a bell, fire a revolver or send up three rockets at five-minute intervals. Automobilists running on country roads at night must send up a red rocket every mile and wait 10 minutes for the road to clear. They then may proceed carefully, blowing their horns and shooting Roman candles.

While such tongue-in-cheek restrictions were never applied, there are some who think perhaps it might have been a good idea. There are some who see the problems of automobile transportation not as a mere nuisance but as actual warfare between the automobile and mankind. One writer claims that the "mortal conflict between cars and cities is intensifying all around the world," pointing to the fact that in the 1960s the automobile population increased 42 percent in our own country. It also increased 130 percent in Europe, and Western Europe now has a greater vehicle density than America. In Latin America, automobiles increased by 150 percent, and in Asia by a surprising 450 percent.

The "vehicle explosion" is all the more remarkable since in 1900 there were only 8,000 automobiles registered in the United States. In just five years the number had climbed to more than 77,000, and by 1915 there were almost 2½ million registered automobiles. This provided a strong enough "lobby" to persuade government to get busy and begin to build roads suitable for rubber-tired gas buggies. In 1916, Woodrow Wilson signed the first federal law to establish a countrywide system of interstate highways. The Federal Highway Act was passed in 1921, and the present system of national and state roads began to grow. There are now about 3 ½ million miles of roads, about 500,000 miles of this within the cities. Gasoline taxes, registration fees, and property taxes provide the bulk of the money needed for maintenance of highways.

In 1970 more than $25 billion was spent by the United States government for transportation development, nearly 85 percent of it for more highways. The great Federal Interstate Highway System added tens of thousands of miles of highways, and additional millions of miles of other roads were upgraded in the quarter-century from 1945 to 1970. Yet only 16 miles of mass-transit lines were built during that time.

Freeways and automobiles are not being forced on unwilling Americans, however. Surveys show that most people are firmly committed to that method of transportation.

The automobile is a key problem. Tied as we are to the benefits and the joys of personal transportation, we find it practically impossible to live without the automobile. At the same time, it is becoming increasingly difficult to live with it. We shall return to our consideration of this crucial problem of society in Chapter 9.

CHAPTER
8

The Age of Flight

Earthbound human beings have dreamed about flying like birds for a long, long time. Some even tried to put their dreams into practice. Ancient writings tell of Chinese, Greek, and other would-be aeronauts who made themselves wings and leaped from high places—usually at great injury to themselves, and sometimes to their deaths. The classic tale of men with wings is the Greek legend of Icarus and Daedalus, in which the former flew too near the sun, melted the bindings of his wings, and plummeted to earth like a stone.

There are other legends of Chinese going aloft in huge kites, and even of an enterprising birdman who added rockets (which the Chinese invented). This first attempt at rocket flight was not particularly successful. Later, Leonardo da Vinci devoted much time and hope to a flapping-wing machine in which he planned to fly like an oversized bird. His own writings make no comment on the test flight that apparently took place. However, the reports of his contemporaries suggest that the flight ended in total failure, with injury to the person and the pride of the great painter-inventor. From that time on, Leonardo made no further mention of human flight in his writings.

Dreamers have notoriously hard heads, and the failures of others seldom discourage them. There was of course much motivation for flying as a means of transportation. Flight would not only provide a thrilling sport but also carry people

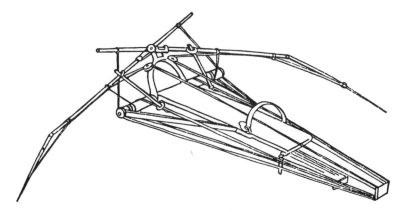

Leonardo da Vinci's ornithopter project.

from Point A to Point B by the most direct route. No longer would travelers have to slog through the mud, scale high mountains, or detour around bodies of water. Aviators could travel "as the crow flies," an expression that is still part of our language. A straight line is the shortest distance between two points, and the human spirit constantly strives for the best way, the shortest route, the fastest method of getting from here to there.

It is possible that some brave and unsung pioneer succeeded in flying before those who historically get credit for the feat. Certainly many inventors have put together "flying machines" and hopped off the handiest high point. But generally it is accepted that two French adventurers named de Rozier and d'Arlandes made the first successful aerial flight. This was in 1783, and their machine was not an airplane but a huge balloon built by the Montgolfier brothers. Not for 108 more years would man fly in a heavier-than-air craft, and then only downhill. In 1891 Otto Lilienthal built and flew his first frail glider in Germany. Lilienthal was the first glider pilot and also the first fatality in such a vehicle. When he crashed in 1896 his last words were, "Sacrifices must be made."

VICTORY AT KITTY HAWK: 1903

Lilienthal's statement was prophetic, for in 1899 the second fatality occurred when England's Percy Pilcher crashed his glider in England. By now, however, a number of men in various countries were soaring through the air. America's Octave Chanute was too old to fly, himself, but he designed and built an excellent biplane glider in which others made 7,100 safe flights, some of them as long as 350 feet. It was from Chanute that the two men generally credited with fathering powered flight took inspiration and began to learn the art.

Orville and Wilbur, the famed Wright Brothers, earned their living building and repairing the bicycles that were then enjoying great popularity. But the Wrights, unlike so many others involved in mechanical work, skipped over the next logical step after the bicycle. Instead of a snorting gas buggy, the Wrights decided to build a flying machine. And they did.

In 1900 the Wrights flew their first glider along the seashore at Kitty Hawk, North Carolina. By 1903 they had built another craft of similar design but with a small gasoline engine mounted between its wings. On December 17 of that year they made the first powered flights in airplane history. The distance of the first flight was only 120 feet, and it lasted just 12 seconds. But the beginning had been made, and before the day was over they accomplished a flight of almost one minute and a distance of about half a mile through the air.

A DREAM DELAYED

It would seem that the Wright brothers would immediately become heroes, driven in an automobile triumphantly down a New York street a foot deep in confetti. Perhaps part of the reason this did not happen was that the automobile itself was taking all the attention of the public. For whatever reason, hardly any notice was taken of the miracle at Kitty Hawk. The Wrights continued to be looked upon as slightly eccentric young bicycle mechanics who ought to be working on a motor car that would have practical value.

By 1905 Orville and Wilbur had progressed to 25-mile flights in their newer machines, averaging nearly 40 miles an hour and demonstrating safe takeoffs and landings plus the ability to navigate wherever they wanted to go. Surely by now they would be famous, with government and industry standing in line waving money for the chance to build these marvelous machines in quantity. Surprisingly, the real situation was just the opposite: absolutely nothing came of the remarkable flights, and the Wrights were so disappointed that they locked up their marvelous machines, ceased experiments, and did no flying for two and a half years.

Not until May of 1908 did airplane flights made by the Wright brothers at last wake up the public to the fact that man could now fly in powered aircraft. Both in the United States and in France (to which country the inventors had turned when their own showed no interest), the brothers made demonstration flights that were almost beyond belief. They carried a passenger on flights lasting more than an hour and flew distances of almost 50 miles at altitudes up to 360 feet. England's Major B. F. S. Baden-Powell stated correctly: "Wilbur Wright is in possession of a power which controls the fate of nations . . ." But this power was not without its price. At military tests in America with Orville at the controls, Lieutenant Thomas E. Selfridge, the passenger, was killed when the plane crashed. Sacrifices continued to be made, as Lilienthal had warned.

THE AGE OF FLIGHT

After the Wrights had shown the way in 1908, it seemed that everybody and his brother built an airplane and flew it. Sisters too, for women became pilots. One of them, Harriet Quimby, suggested that planes could carry passengers between adjacent towns, even for distances of 50 or 60 miles. Shortly after her startling statement, however, Miss Quimby was killed in a plane crash. Aviation casualties continued, and usually they were more spectacular than transport accidents on the ground. In 1910 the first midair crash of aircraft occurred. Such accidents continued to plague these new craft moving in three dimensions, often in bad weather or in the dark of night. Despite the remarkable success of aircraft, skeptics and critics managed to enjoy themselves. Even those who should have known better joined in. One noted scientist commented:

> The popular mind often pictures gigantic flying machines speeding across the Atlantic carrying innumerable passengers in a way analogous to our modern steamships. It seems safe to say that such ideas are wholly visionary, and even if a machine could get across with one or two passengers, the expense would be prohibitive to any but the capitalist who could use his own yacht. Another fallacy is to suppose that the flying machine could be used to drop dynamite upon an enemy in time of war.

That gentleman must have forgotten Dionysus Lardner's earlier ridiculing of the idea that steamships could sail the Atlantic. Unfortunately it had to be recorded that the dropping of dynamite came before commercial service over the oceans.

In the meantime, more modest aerial vehicles were getting started. Zeppelin "dirigibles" flew between Berlin, Frankfort, Hamburg, and Dresden. Passengers sat in lightweight wicker chairs in a roomy cabin and were served complimentary wine during the flights. Before World War I ended such service, the big gas bags had made 1,600 scheduled flights, covering about 100,000 miles with no serious mishaps. Airplanes and flying boats also carried passengers. America's first airline operated from Tampa to St. Petersburg in Florida, covering the twenty-two miles in only twenty minutes.

This must have required officials to look tactfully the other way. A few years earlier, Florida lawmakers copied the approach taken in restricting automobiles and passed laws limiting the speeds of planes flying over a city. At ten feet, planes had to fly 8 miles per hour; at twenty feet, 15 mph; at fifty feet, 30 mph. Aviators were forbidden to fly more than 50 mph. Planes also had to have horns on them, air brakes, and parachutes to lower them in case the engines failed!

An earlier critic had said planes would never drop bombs. After World War I, during which many bombs *were* dropped, America's Billy Mitchell was eventually court-martialed for suggesting—and then proving—that a bomber could knock out a battleship. The then Secretary of the Navy boasted that he would stand bareheaded on the deck of any target battleship. Luckily he was not in that position when Mitchell's bombers hit and sank a German battleship in twenty-five minutes. Five other warships were also sunk. The airplane had beaten the battleship decisively; later it would vanquish the mighty passenger lines that had long held a monopoly on travel across the oceans. But that took a little while.

World War I had improved the airplane and accelerated its progress. No sooner were hostilities over than Navy flying boats succeeded in crossing the Atlantic, to the great embarrassment of the scientist who had said it could not be done. Airships also crossed the Atlantic as early as 1919, and for a time it seemed that they were ideal for passenger service, a dream that would later end in tragic finality with the explosion and burning of Germany's dirigible *Hindenburg* in America.

TRIALS OF AIR TRANSPORT

By 1921 America had eighty-two operating airlines. But there were also 1,200 airplane accidents that year, and by 1923 only seventeen commercial airlines remained. Even war ace Eddie Rickenbacker got out of the aviation business and into the safer field of car manufacturing. Nevertheless, aviation kept improving until it began living up to the "wild claims" made by its backers. In 1922 an Army plane flew across the country with only one stop, making the trip in 21 hours. The pilot's name was James Doolittle. By 1923 a German-built transport plane flown by U.S. Army pilots traveled nonstop from California to New York in 27 hours, and a year later an Army single-seater flew from New York to San Francisco between dawn and dusk.

Even Henry Ford, who was still leading the way in auto-making, got into aviation. His tri-motored aluminum transport plane, nicknamed the *Tin Goose*, became a standard for American airlines and eventually flew all over the world. A few of those planes still fly.

Airmail had long been a dream of the Post Office, and experiments began as early as 1918. However, on the first attempt everything went wrong. First, the stamps were printed upside down. The mechanics took hours to get the engine started on the Curtis "Jenny," and when finally the plane took off, the pilot went the wrong way. The air mail landed in a remote part of Maryland, came back to Washington, D.C. in a car, and went to New York on a train. With regularly operating airlines in the 1920s the government issued contracts for the carrying of mail by plane, and first-class service was cut from several days to one day across the country.

In 1927 young Charles Lindbergh flew nonstop and alone from New York to Paris, demonstrating not just his own courage but the dependability of the single engine that powered his *Spirit of St. Louis*. A female "Lindy," Amelia Earhart, flew the Atlantic in 1928. But she died trying to fly the Pacific in 1937. In 1931 Wiley Post flew around the world in about eight days and a half. Two years later, flying alone and in a weird "pressure suit" for high altitude flight, Post cut his record to seven days and a quarter. He and humorist Will Rogers later crashed and died during a flight over Alaska.

By 1929 Pan American Airways was flying 44 of its "flying boat" aircraft on North American and South American coastal routes, getting valuable experience for the soon-to-come ocean flights. And in 1936 the *China Clipper* began carrying passengers across the mighty Pacific.

The Spirit of St. Louis, in which Col. Charles A. Lindbergh flew from New York to Paris in May, 1927. *U.S. Air Force Photo.*

Then Donald Douglas began producing his famous "DC" transports, craft that could fly three miles a minute. The airline "hostess" was making plane travel more popular than ever, and "sleeper planes" were operating for those who wished to cross the continent in ultimate comfort. Meals were served aloft, and air travel became the glamorous and exciting way to go. Once, the Wright brothers had amazed the world by flying 360 feet above the ground in their frail biplanes. Now pressurized airliners operated regularly in the stratosphere at speeds of 250 miles an hour.

At that point the second World War intervened, and air transport took time out again to haul supplies and to drop dynamite, plus atomic bombs. When peace came, aviation had progressed to even higher levels of performance. There were thousands of the workhorse DC-3s left over, and many of these are still plodding the skies today. They quickly gave way to DC-4s, DC-6s, and DC-7s. But it was becoming apparent that the propeller-driven airplane was in need of a replacement. A reciprocating engine in an airplane is a complicated device, so complicated that many wonder how it operates at all. The jet engine is far simpler, yet it took aviation engineers many decades to produce a successful one. World War II was a great incentive, and it was England's Frank Whittle who did the trick.

THE COMING OF THE JETS

Propeller-driven craft were moving through the sky at 500 miles an hour, a fantastic speed still not believed by many critics of aviation. But that seemed to be the limit for conventional engines. A new powerplant was needed to push toward 600 miles an hour, and Whittle's jet did that in the 1930s. His country was being bombed by German rockets traveling so fast that conventional fighter aircraft could not catch them to shoot them down. But the jet-powered *Gloster Meteor* flew faster than 500 miles an hour and caught the V-1 rockets. In America, Lockheed produced the P-80 *Shooting Star* for use in our air war.

When gold was discovered in California in 1849, it took a month to cross the country. A century later, pilot William Council blazed across the country in a P-80 in just over four hours. The most important work of jet aircraft came after the war was over and commercial transport picked up where it had left off. The "jet age" of air transportation began in 1952, when British Overseas Airways inaugurated service between London and Rome. A scheduled speed of 500 miles an hour was offered by the pioneering *Comet* jetliner, and America suddenly lost her supremacy of the airways. However, structural problems hit the fast-flying jet craft. They began to break apart in the air at high altitudes in tragic accidents that killed many passengers. Because of this unfortunate setback for England, America's Boeing 707 jets took over. Soon air travelers were hearing their pilot announce flight altitude of

Lockheed P-80 in flight. *U.S. Air Force Photo.*

40,000 feet and a speed of 600 miles an hour. Before long the jets had a virtual monopoly on long-distance air travel and were even profitable on short hauls. Society sprouted a traveling fringe called "the jet set." Today it is almost impossible to find a propeller-driven commercial airliner.

In 1914 a man with far more accurate foresight than many scientists said of the airplane: "First Europe, and then the globe, will be linked by flight, and the nations so knit together that they will grow to be next-door neighbors. This conquest of the air will prove ultimately, to be man's greatest conquest and most glorious triumph. What railways have done for nations, airways will do for the world."

In Jules Verne's *Around the World in Eighty Days*, written just a century ago, Phineas Fogg managed the trip on boat, train, motor car, and balloon. Since that fictional voyage, reporters have occasionally repeated this circling of the globe. In 1924, a voyage by Army planes still took more than 140 days. But by 1936 three reporters made it on scheduled commercial flights, on the dirigible *Hindenburg*, and in the flying boat *China Clipper*, in just 15 days. Today it is possible to fly around the world in commercial jet planes in just two days at an average speed of 500 miles an hour, forty times as fast as the dashing Mr. Fogg.

At the close of World War II it was noted that transportation advances had made the entire world smaller, measured by travel time, than the original thirteen colonies of America. Today a further shrinkage has been accomplished. Jetliners have in effect reduced the world to about a third the size of the colonies. But it is not only in intercontinental travel that the airplane rules. In the United States, airlines carried nearly half the domestic passenger traffic, almost as much as railroads and buses combined.

Early in its development the airplane demonstrated that it could carry heavy loads. Sadly, much of that weight has been in the form of bombs and other war weapons, but airplanes have also hauled coal (in the "cold war" days when Berlin was besieged by the Russians) and such heavy loads as mining machinery. Today helicopters carry power-line towers into remote areas and also airlift small buildings to their sites. Air freight is a growing business, and airplanes have even carried huge guided missiles across the country from factory to launch pad. Airmail is freight, and we willingly pay a few cents more for the great speed of the jet. But air freight now includes such bulky cargo as books, baked goods, fruits, and clothes.

The "jumbo jets" have worked well, and air travel continues to be the best-run and most convenient transportation available. Even the ancient dreams of pleasure palaces aloft have come true, with color movies, stereo music, piano bars, and excellent foods at reasonable fares. Ironically a major problem of air travel is the traffic jam on the ground. Getting to and from airports often takes longer than the flight from airport to airport. The new crime of "skyjacking" presently poses a threat to aviation, but it seems that this will eventually be solved. Air travel is too important to be halted by a new version of the age-old crime of piracy.

"HIGH FLIGHT"

In the United States there are about 2,500 airliners. There are also an additional 100,000 "private" craft. There are more than a million licensed pilots in the United States. Compared with automobile drivers, this is a handful, but the percentage is growing. Whether or not flying will ever be the ultimate "personal transport" is questionable. There have been attempts to market *Flying Flea* designs and other such craft that would give everyone wings. The autogiro and the helicopter are also attempts in that direction. In comic strips of many years ago, Buck Rogers flew with a "rocket belt." This science-fiction device became reality more than a decade ago, and some daring pilots have flown as high as a hundred feet with such contraptions.

It is doubtful that aviation pioneers went at their work with the idea of transporting people or goods at high speed for pay. Most enthusiasts thought first of the joy of aerial flight. That joy persists in the private flying that flourishes today. Perhaps the finest expression of the sheer beauty of flight is the poem "High Flight," written during World War II by John Gillespie Magee, Jr., a young Canadian cadet who was later killed in a flying accident.

The author flying his Phoebus C sailplane.

    . . . Up, up the long delirious, burning blue
I've topped the windswept heights with easy grace,
    Where never lark, or even eagle flew.

Flying is not just a business. It is a sport, also, and there are
tens of thousands of planes used for that purpose. Learning to
fly is fun, like learning to ski, surf, or drive a ski-mobile.
Flight is freedom in three dimensions instead of only two; it is
travel high above the world, a sensation that can be ap-
proached only in such pursuits as skin-diving.

For some, the ultimate in flying is soaring flight in a high-
performance craft without an engine. Such sailplanes have
made flights of more than 900 miles, climbed eleven miles
high, and traveled faster than 200 miles an hour. Today, there
is renewed interest in lightweight gliders, and many young
people are launching themselves from nearby hills much as
the Wright brothers did seventy years ago.

THE SST AND BEYOND

The jet engine pushed airplane speeds to about the speed of
sound. Here was a bitter pill for those who a generation
earlier had protested that twenty miles an hour would boil the
blood, asphyxiate passengers, and cause terrible diseases of
the brain. But even Mach 1 was not fast enough for engineers
and designers. The X-1 rocket plane pushed past the speed of
sound in 1947; twenty years later the X-15 had exceeded
4,000 miles an hour, almost Mach 7! In the meantime, the Air
Force B-58 *Hustler* in 1956 demonstrated a speed of Mach 2.
And in the 1960s North American Aviation produced the XB-
70 bomber for the Air Force. That weird, needle-nosed craft
traveled at 2,000 miles and hour and ushered in the age of
flight in the range of Mach 3. It was only natural that
designers begin thinking of such craft for passenger travel.

Again the critics got busy. Who in his right mind needed to
fly *faster than sound*? The same men who had argued against
the coming of jet travel now used the jets to fly across the

country to argue at meetings against the SST. As a result, instead of the SST, America produced the "jumbo jet" a plane carrying as many as five hundred passengers at the standard 600 miles an hour. England, which had lost its supremacy of the skies, got busy on an SST design in conjunction with France. The result was the *Concorde*, a Mach 2 craft. The U.S.S.R. was slightly ahead of the Europeans with its own SST, the Mach 2 Tu-144.

The Concorde supersonic airliner, jointly designed, developed, and produced by the British and French.

As work went on with the *Concorde* design, the temptation was too much for designers in the United States. The North American, Lockheed, and Boeing firms all began to design such craft. Boeing won design competitions and government subsidies were granted toward building America's first SST. A story in Seattle's *Post-Intelligencer* gave a hint of the tremendous speed promised by the new generation of air transport: "In a supersonic plane, flying at 1,900 miles an hour, 495 miles will speed by as the passenger drinks a glass of champagne. One hors d'oeuvre will consume 16.5 miles; entree and wine, 1,485 miles; and a cup of coffee, 333 miles."

But the project was destined to fail before it got much past the drawing board. Mach 3 aircraft produce noisy and sometimes damaging "sonic booms," and there was much resistance to these. Some scientists feared that a fleet of SSTs would drastically change the composition of the atmosphere by destroying ozone, add CO_2 which would heat up the environment, and subject passengers to too much cosmic radiation. Innocent victims on the ground not only would be blasted by sonic booms but might be subjected to increased risk of skin cancer from ultraviolet ray exposure. As a result of all the furore, plus the huge sums of subsidy money involved, the government terminated the SST project.

Russia, England, and France continue their work toward commercial SST travel. The next few years will tell what is going to happen. It seems doubtful that air transportation has really hit a barrier it can't overcome, for even before the SST controversy, designers were planning Mach 5 and even Mach 8, HST's, or hypersonic transports. The "ballistic" airliner, literally fired at its destination, could bring the day when any spot on earth would be within three hours.

Designers are working on the sonic boom problem and some think it can be satisfactorily solved. Fears of overheating the atmosphere or triggering diseases may prove to be groundless. If SST service by the *Concorde* and the Tu-144 is successful, it is possible that the United States will get back to work on its Mach 3 SST, which would travel about 600 miles an hour faster than the *Concorde*. The next decade will decide whether the end has been reached in airliner speed, or if we will move on to link the world even more closely.

CHAPTER
9

Urban Transit

We live in a remarkable age of transportation. A passenger can be carried around the world in two days in comfort of a kind only dreamed of a century ago. We can cross the entire width of our country in about four hours. Yet sometimes we take that long getting to and from work only a few miles from home. This is the problem of urban transportation, the "mass transit" mess that is a prime topic of conversation these days, around our dinner tables and in top-level meetings in Washington, D. C.

Transportation can carry men to the moon and back at rapid speed, and most of our long trips are accomplished with great dispatch. With the scrapping of the SST we have decided for the moment that 600 miles an hour is sufficient even for long distances. Six hundred miles in an hour is certainly not a bad pace. That's ten miles in a single minute, a speed that the cranks of old would have had a field day with. If 30 miles an hour would afflict passengers with *delirium fu-riosum*, surely twenty times that speed would kill them instantly.

Instead of mental problems resulting from traveling ten miles a minute, however, most of us suffer them from taking far too many minutes to travel ten miles, a good round number for many of the trips we must make in the pursuit of modern urban and suburban life. In rush hours on a freeway designed for 70-mile-an-hour travel, it sometimes takes more than an hour to go the ten miles a jet liner overhead travels in just 60 seconds. Researchers say that average speed on city streets today is no better than it was in the old days of horse- back and carriage transport. Often it is worse. Something is obviously wrong if urban transit is our biggest problem in moving people today. We seem to have succeeded with the big tasks and failed miserably on the little ones.

LIFE IN THE CITY

Urban transit was not much of a problem in man's first cities. According to the noted city planner C. A. Doxiadis, early city dwellers could go anywhere they had to go in the community in about ten minutes of walking. A brisk walk will cover nearly a mile in that time, and cities seldom got bigger than that. When they finally did, residents often needed a horse for their trips. Later came the omnibus, coach, carriage, or whatever other vehicle was locally popular.

Not all our ancestors were city dwellers. In fact, most of them lived in rural areas. For one reason and another, however, they found it necessary or desirable to visit the city from time to time. Another rule of thumb quoted by Doxiadis is that most people wanted to live within a day's walk of the city. This meant a distance of about thirty miles, a hike that would wear out most of us, accustomed as we are to motor travel.

There must have been a time when urban transit was what we would now wistfully consider ideal. There are still a few places even today where that pleasant, uncrowded condition prevails. But in general the cities grew crowded with normal population increase, industrialization, and the urge of rural people to "move to town" rather than remain in the country. To take care of this growth and at the same time keep the city small enough to get around in, buildings were made taller and jammed closer together. Streets were laid out rigidly, generally in the familiar north-south, east-west grid. For a time this helped, but over the years transportation became a major problem Big cities were not only densely populated but also many miles across.

Although it is easy to get that impression today, few people travel in the city just for fun. It is certainly not that rewarding. Most people are simply trying to get from Point A to Point B for a variety of purposes. In ancient times a farmer worked on the land he owned or rented and lived there too. Trips to church or meeting house were the extent of his regular travel. Today few of us are fortunate enough to work at home. Many travel long distances to and from work, others commute to school. Still others are shopping, paying bills, going to see the doctor or dentist, attending a funeral, visiting the hair dresser, or meeting a friend.

As cities grew it was more and more the case that workmen lived some distance from their place of employment, and that students were not just a block or two from school. Often the facilities for recreation were on the other side of town. Horses and buggies began to crowd the streets about the theater, railroad station, courthouse, or neighborhood park. Long before automobiles, things got so bad that traffic laws had to be drawn up and enforced.

The coming of the bicycle was a blessing, and for a time the two-wheeler eased the traffic problem. A bicycle takes much less space and is far more maneuverable than a horse and buggy. In some cities, notably Copenhagen, bike travel came to be—and still is—a popular form of urban transport. The bicycle could not do it all, of course, and there continued to be buggies and carriages, stagecoaches, and omnibuses. We consider present-day traffic jams so terrible because we can't remember what it was like on a narrow, muddy street jammed with humanity and great numbers of horse-drawn vehicles.

Even in early days there was some commuting from outside the city to work or for business appointments. The railroad and the streetcar eased this transit problem, and in time an effective commuter network evolved. As traffic on the street level became unbearable, mass transit went underground or above it. The subways in London, built against great opposition, have since repaid the effort a thousandfold and more. One unexpected bonus was the saving of countless lives during World War II bombing raids. The subway tunnels proved to be very safe shelters. Overhead, the elevated railways speeded schedules but also defaced the environment and deafened those unfortunates living close by. The conventional elevated railroad tracks were supplanted by neater and quieter "monorails," especially in Europe.

THE SYSTEM BREAKS DOWN

In time, the streetcar gave way to the safer and more flexible bus. By the time these vehicles were available, so was the ultimate in personal transit, the automobile. It was the automobile that brightened the commuter's life and at the same time threw a monkey wrench into the creaky machinery of urban transit. This came about for basic psychological reasons. Humans value freedom and privacy highly, and they had given up the horse and buggy only for faster travel in public vehicles. Speed they prized, but they did not appreciate the resulting loss of flexibility and choice. Subway trains hauled workers quickly to and from their jobs, but they were deafeningly noisy, crowded, smelly, and as time went on, actually dangerous. In short, mass transport was dehumanizing and humans tolerated it only when they had no choice. When an alternative came along they grabbed it like drowning victims clutching at a life preserver. The automobile became king of the road.

In New York City, and in some other big cities, urban transit has continued much as it was in the old days. With the city so jammed with buses, taxis and people, only a bold man ventures out in his own automobile. There are a few such brave and hardy spirits but not many. The private automobile has not captured New York City simply because it cannot. Commuters are trapped into riding the buses, subways, or taxis because there is no alternative but walking. Some do that, of course, but there are times when the weather will not cooperate.

Population seems to be the key to mass transit in public conveyances. Where there is not the density of a New York, London, Montreal, Chicago, or Tokyo, public transit weakens and dies because it does not have a sufficient captive market. We have noted the death of the Pacific Electric system in and around Los Angeles. In earlier days it was also possible to ride the streetcar from San Diego all the way to La Jolla, and a pleasant trip it was. The same with the picturesque Coronado Island Ferry, long used by nearly everyone who had to commute, and by many who were just sightseeing. But recently a great bridge was built to span the Bay and the old ferryboats were retired, like the majestic steamboats of an earlier era on the Mississippi.

Today a popular argument is whether it was the automobile that wrecked urban transit, or urban transit itself. Poor service really killed the buses and trains, some say. Why should anyone put up with that when he can commute much more pleasantly in his own vehicle? If transit companies had provided good service at a reasonable price most commuters would have continued to use them, they say.

On the other hand, urban transit people disagree strongly. They could not improve service as passengers and fares became fewer, and a snowballing of cause and effect led to the terrible sickness, and in some cases the actual death, of urban transit. This argument seems to have much truth in it, for even when excellent service has been offered to commuters—including door-to-door pick-up and delivery, music and snacks aboard the bus, and the like—there has still been no increase of transit passengers.

THE CHALLENGE OF "URBAN SPRAWL"

Particularly has the abandonment of urban transit been evident in areas of "urban sprawl" such as southern California. Californians, many of them refugees from the crowded conditions of the east, decided to build their cities out instead of up. Land was cheap for outlying subdivisions and there were good roads to town. Who minded driving ten miles to work—or twenty, or even fifty? On the new freeways, that was less than hour each way, and a pleasant trip with the car radio or tape deck for company and entertainment. As urban sprawl continued, it had a side effect that was little noticed at first: those who wanted and needed urban transit found it less available or not available at all in the new life style.

Traditionally, easterners had commuted for long distances. Many working in New York City lived by choice in pleasant New England cities and towns fifty and more miles away. Commuting was little problem: drive to the station (in a stationwagon, of course) and ride a fast train to work. The service was fast and economical; passengers could read, work, visit, relax or even sleep.

Such service required a "mainline." These corridors exist around New York, Chicago, and a few other cities. At first, such developments took place around Los Angeles and led to an efficient commuter railroad system. But later on, the Angelenos began to fan out all over the countryside. Not to every point of the compass, of course, for Los Angeles was not that far from the ocean. But to the north, east, south, and all points in between, new subdivisions developed. Highways and freeways were built with government money. But no new tracks were laid for commuter trains. Instead, old ones were torn up.

There were buses of course, and some people rode them. But the buses were subject to the same traffic tieups as cars. Instead of riding the bus why not drive yourself? Again, there was the convenient flexibility of personal transport. One could shop or do errands on the way to and from work, an impossibility with public transit. A bus route also meant a rigid time schedule in addition to a fixed route. Meanwhile, the fares continued to climb.

Mass transit works well when it has a large volume of business on a few lines, but urban sprawl spread potential commuters over a great area. No transit company could afford to provide frequent service to everywhere at a price cheaper than personal transport. Gradually the service declined. As few people rode a certain route, Schedules were cut and even fewer passengers paid fares. Franchises often forced transit lines to continue runs that carried few passengers and lost money.

THE AIRPORT BOTTLENECK

One of the biggest urban transit woes is carrying air travelers to and from the airport. Ground transport generally picks up and lets off its passengers downtown, close to where they want to go. Airports originated in fields at the edge of town, and they have moved farther out all the time. It is no exaggeration to say (although it now sounds like a broken record) that many air travelers spend more time riding to and from airports than in the air. Of course, they still save time by air travel, but how much better it would be if the surface portion could be made as speedy and pleasant as the flight itself.

Some cities have set aside high-speed special lanes for commuter buses to airports. The most advanced system yet tried is the "Sky Lounge." This picks up passengers in a special bus, which is then airlifted by helicopter to the airport. Back on its own wheels, it takes passengers right to their planes. Tokyo, whose Tokkaido Line trains are a great success, has not always been as successful in efforts to improve transportation. For example, a new monorail was built to take people from the city to the airport, but hardly anyone uses it.

THE MASS TRANSIT MESS

Anyone who isn't aware of the mass transit mess has been asleep for two decades, or at least is completely out of touch with the real world. For a few rural dwellers, there is still no problem. But most of us live in cities now, and the percentage continues to increase so that the next generation will practically all be urban dwellers unless some dramatic and perhaps drastic changes take place.

Our freeways, very efficient between cities, are increasingly choked with traffic in and around the cities. Cars inch along bumper to bumper, fouling the air with their fumes and the curses of angry drivers. Accidents are common, particularly in bad weather. More and more of our time is spent just getting to and from work. Once billboards advertised new subdivisions "only minutes from town." But minutes quickly make hours, commuters are learning, and far too many hours are spent in tedious trips on "expressways" that for the most part seem very poorly named.

Even worse is the plight of the inner city dwellers, particularly the poor. It is an almost unbelievable fact that there are people today who do not own automobiles. For some few, this is by choice, for most it is economic lack. They simply do not have enough money to purchase and maintain a car, then continually pay for gasoline, road tolls, license fees, property taxes, insurance, and all the rest. Another segment of society cannot drive for physical reasons. So a sizable percentage of city dwellers must rely on public transport to get to work, to shop, to go to church or school, or for recreation. Increasingly these people are finding only poor service available, and in some cases no service at all. Such a paralysis of movement is a factor in the dying of inner cities.

The straw that breaks the camel's back is that while many see their means of getting about slowly dying on its tracks, their environment has been blighted with asphalt and concrete. On these "freeways" are clogged seas of noisy, dirty vehicles that choke the air. It is hard to accept the fact that the mass transit system has failed. But in many particulars it has, even though industry continues to operate, and its workers somehow manage to struggle home and get back in time for tomorrow's shift.

CAN WE GET THERE FROM HERE?

Over the past few decades, the many levels of government have poured billions of dollars into transportation. Second only to education in dollars spent domestically, this service is so vital that a Department of Transportation was created—belatedly, many critics say. Most individuals spend more of their money getting from one place to another than they do for anything else. Many of us spend more money for our automobiles than for any other item on the budget—more than for our home, or food, or education. It is a remarkable fact, and the more so because most of us are unaware of transportation costs. But then travel is almost as much a habit as breathing, and we seldom stop to think about taking a breath.

An ever-increasing share of our taxes is being spent on road-building. As the results become more obvious, some people rise up and protest loudly against the pourers of concrete blotting out San Francisco, New Orleans, and other once-charming cities. The net result, besides, seems to be little more than monumental traffic jams, terrible pollution, and more fatalities on the highways despite the promise that freeways would reduce such casualties. Perhaps the biggest gripe of all is that planners seem not to know that there is any other way to go but by automobile.

In response to the clamor, and also to the obvious fact that something is wrong, government (again belatedly in the eyes of many) has turned its attention and some of its money to the urban transit problem. Grants and loans are at last being made to ailing bus lines and other forms of local transportation. Many cities have had to take over bankrupt private systems and often to operate them at a loss. For many critics, such subsidies are like feeding a dead horse, something even more ridiculous than beating such an animal. Buggy whips are seldom made anymore, because there is no call for them. The advocates of automobiles use the same argument against urban transit: it failed because it wasn't needed or wanted.

In fairness, it must be repeated that when trial runs were made, little interest seemed evident. For example, the city of Phoenix, saddled with a bankrupt transit system, tested a supplementary line offering fares below cost. When its passengers were added to those of the existing line, the total was only about what it had been before addition of the new line.

Suggestions that part of the money taken from automobile drivers as taxes be used to subsidize urban transit have been met with screams of outrage. And indeed such protests seem to make sense. Why should the automobile driver, who is already paying for the highways, and even contributing a part of his money to such things as school funds, be forced to "give free rides" to bus passengers—especially when it seems impossible to get people on the buses anyway?

The air has become thick with charges and countercharges, almost as blue with confusion as with smog. Pointing to the success of New York and, particularly, Montreal, proponents argue for subways even in places where urban sprawl prevails. In spite of evidence that only a high population density, or a corridor like that down the eastern seaboard, can support such mass transit systems, some proponents continue to insist on them, and to vilify the highway builders for continuing their work.

It is an unfortunate fact that just excavating for a subway costs millions of dollars a mile, and that to satisfy the demand in an area of urban sprawl billions of dollars would be required for the many lines radiating out from a center and also going crosstown. Add to this the cost of tracks, switching equipment, signaling devices, and computerized automation, and even the national debt begins to look like a modest sum. Furthermore, having built this magnificent urban transit system, we might find that its cars often ran with only a few passengers and sometimes with none at all. Because of our love for the automobile, we have set ourselves a problem with no easy solution. In short, we may not be able to get there from here with conventional mass transit.

BART, the magnificent Bay Area Rapid Transit system, links outlying areas to San Francisco.

New Ways to Go

One new transit system is being watched with great interest. This is BART, the magnificent Bay Area Rapid Transit system linking outlying areas with San Francisco, whose irate citizens some years ago put a stop to freeways that threatened to obliterate the city. A completely new system, with the most modern controls and equipment, and attractive cars and stations, BART is a multibillion-dollar project that was and still is very controversial. Surprisingly, BART is the first new rapid transit system in seventy years. It will operate over seventy-five miles of track in three counties, and critics claim that it is too oriented to the suburban commuter and too little to the bulk of commuters, the people living and working in San Francisco.

Washington, D.C., has begun a 98-mile subway system that will cost $3 billion or more, linking Maryland and Virginia with Washington. Atlanta, too, has tackled the rapid-transit problem and is building a fifty-mile rail system, nine miles of it underground.

For years many transit systems have been operating at a loss, with the difference made up in government subsidies. Some authorities argue that the best solution is to go all the way and make public transportation free, just as the streets and parks are free. There is no free anything, of course, and what is really suggested is that mass transit be paid for out of taxes and used by anyone as much or as little as needed. Along this line, Chicago's Transit Authority is considering banning automobiles from the downtown area and substituting a free transit system—if the state and Federal governments will help pay for it. There are some places around the country where cars have not been allowed for a long time. One of these is Mackinac Island in Michigan. However, that is a recreation area and not a busy city with a living to earn.

There has been renewed interest in the bicycle as a means of mass transit, and in many cities bike paths and lanes are being provided or at least considered. Here is a way to bridge the gap between vehicle transit and walking, for many trips are too long for footpower but not long enough to justify two tons of steel and glass.

More exotic systems like moving streets or sidewalks have been proposed and may become reality in shopping malls, government complexes, and large plants. We already have public elevators and escalators. Lay them out horizontally, it is suggested, and provide free urban transit. This elevator analogy may not be a good one, since the elevator seems the end of all personal freedom. People have been trapped in elevators; some will not even enter them because they suffer from claustrophobia when cooped up in such a small area with many other people.

The clean, economical bicycle is becoming more and more popular as a means of transit. *AMF Incorporated.*

THE MATTER OF EFFICIENCY

About one motor vehicle in six is not an automobile but a truck or a bus. In fact, about seven million Americans make their living driving trucks and buses. This gives an idea of the size of the motor transport industry. Motor vehicles carry an appreciable amount of the nation's freight and passengers. School buses are a common sight, and there are many buses in local public transit. Others carry passengers between cities, on business, vacation, or visits about the country. A single bus holds as many people as twenty or more automobiles but of course does not offer the flexibility and freedom we hold so dear.

Just as there is great variety in types of transportation, there is also a great difference in terms of passenger-carrying efficiency. For example, an ocean liner like the *Queen Mary* has a "net propulsion efficiency" of about 7, just about that of a four-passenger cabin yacht. Net propulsion efficiency means the number of passenger-miles produced from one gallon of fuel. At the other end of the scale are vehicles like the Volkswagen Microbus, which with seven passengers yields a net propulsion efficiency of 180. This is about five times the efficiency of a conventional automobile carrying two passengers. Motorcycles also offer great efficiency in the use of fuel, and a new generation of travelers has taken to these. Buses and trains deliver propulsion efficiencies ranging up to 140 passenger-miles per gallon of fuel, but only a relative handful of Americans travel in these vehicles.

People seem tightly tied to their automobiles, however, and perhaps we had better not attempt to part them forcibly. Instead, we might make the automobile fit better into the mass transit concept. Some steps have been taken in this direction, and the Alden "Starr Car" and Cornell University's "Urbmobile" are interesting examples. These small personal vehicles can operate either on streets on their rubber tires, or on tracks with metal wheels mounted between the tires. Drivers could leave home in their own car and drive to the nearest automated freeway. At their destination they would leave the freeway and go about their business without needing to take a bus, call a cab, or walk.

SOLVING THE PEOPLE-MOVING PROBLEM

A dictator would have little trouble solving the transit problem: he would simply select the system he thought would best do the job, and order his subjects to use it. They would comply, go to jail, or suffer otherwise. Fortunately we do not have a dictator; unfortunately our great freedom of choice makes our transit problem far more difficult than it would be if we were more easily satisfied.

Psychologists point out that locomotion is a basic human need, but that man wants to provide, or at least control, that locomotion himself. When this wish is thwarted, as when people are put into prison or have to stay in a hospital for any length of time, all sorts of frustrations arise. So when travelers are thrown in with anyone and everyone in a transit system over which they have no control, they suffer in similar fashion. An example is the sad plight of immigrants coming to America in steerage class on ships. This was almost inhuman travel, tolerated only for the reward at the end of the trip. No one travels in discomfort unless there is no other choice.

In spite of all this, critics claim, transit planners continue to treat human passengers as so many head of cattle or tons of grain to be hauled from one point to another. Most people won't sit still for that sort of handling. In one classic case humans complained that they were being treated more poorly than pigs! Freight trains loaded with hogs could pass directly through Chicago on a long trip, yet humans had to transfer from one station to another. Or they did until they made so much noise that the railroads provided through travel without the troublesome transfer.

It has been suggested that since people travel because of demands put on them by society—work, socializing, recreation, and so on—we should redesign society, including its cities, so that less travel will be needed. This is a possible solution but can be tried easily only in completely new cities or towns. And whether or not we are strong enough to break with the transportation traditions of the last few decades is questionable. More likely we must reach some compromise solution.

Transportation is one of the greatest challenges facing us today, and this problem will only increase in the future. With the trend to more and more urbanization, it is also obvious that urban transit is where the action is. The battle is going to be a big one but we will win it somehow, simply because we must win if we want to keep moving. And man has never quit moving yet.

CHAPTER
10

The Future of Transportation

Transportation has an assured future as long as there are people. Since it seems almost inevitable that there will be even more human beings as time goes on, with more leisure and more money to spend, transportation should flourish even more than it does at present. Considering the existing problems in and around cities, that is a frightening prospect. If we are to enjoy traveling in the years ahead it is obvious that changes will have to made.

Transportation for the next generation will be a blend of the familiar and the new, the commonplace and the startling. It is generally predicted that the automobile will continue to be number one in our hearts and on the nation's streets and highways. Coming on fast, and probably making more progress than any other form of travel, will be air transportation. Rail travel will still be with us, although perhaps very different in form from what we are used to.

In 1950 the automobile carried slightly more than 86 percent of all intercity passenger traffic, and by 1970 the percentage had not changed. That remarkable stability in automobile travel indicates the firm place of that vehicle in the transportation scheme. Buses carried about 55 percent in 1950, but their share declined to just slightly more than 2 percent in 1970. Railroads lost an even greater share, dropping from 66 percent in 1940 to less than 1 percent in 1970.

Airlines increased their share of intercity passenger traffic from 2 percent to 10 percent.

Most travel will obviously be done on these three major transport systems, although some of them may change considerably from the form we are familiar with now. There also may be some revolutionary means of getting from Point A to Point B. In considering tomorrow's transportation we will begin with the familiar and highly prized automobile.

DRIVING INTO TOMORROW

For all the diligent efforts by advocates of mass transit, we will most likely cling tenaciously to our personal means of transportation. Rising population, increasing affluence, and a probable reduction in driving age all will contribute to an even larger number of vehicles on the road in the future than at present. Having tried buses, trains, subways, helicopters, car pools, bicycles, and moving sidewalks with little improvement in the situation, the nation's transportation planners will eventually decide that if they can't beat the automobile they had better join it and try to better match it to our needs.

War is being waged on automobile pollution, and some progress has been made. Smog-control devices are standard on newer cars, and in general there is such a short lifespan for automobiles that improved designs quickly predominate on the highways. There may be drastic changes coming in the type of engine used. The internal-combustion engine, in addition to being inefficient and a polluter, has mechanical problems too, stemming from the fact that its pistons slam back and forth thousands of times a minute. It seems that designers will turn toward rotary engines in the decades ahead. There is even a chance that the steam engine, brought up to date, may prove the Stanley Steamer partisans right and take over a share of the automotive field.

However, there is much evidence to point to the electric motor as the ideal power plant for our streets and highways.

Electric cars were cruising silently and cleanly seventy years ago, and much improvement has been made since then. The electric motor may be linked with the gas or liquid fuel cell to produce electric power directly at a much higher efficiency rate than the internal-combustion engine or steam engine delivers. And electricity is the most convenient form of power for moving vehicles along the automated highways that seem sure to come.

The shortcoming that killed off the early electric car was its short range. However, if the electric car of tomorrow spends much of its time cruising along an electrified highway, refueling will seldom be necessary, making electrics more attractive than automobiles that must stop every few hundred miles.

Actually our highways will be the last travel medium to be equipped with automatic controls for handling the traffic that moves over them. Long ago the railroads shifted from manual control to electric—and then electronic—systems for faster and safer operation. The airlines use the most advanced automatic controls in existence, so accurate that they can be relied on to guide airliners carrying hundreds of passengers through clouds and even to make landings in "zero-zero" weather. Ships, too, are fitted with navigational aids such as radar, loran, shoran, and collision-avoidance equipment. It makes sense that automobiles, which carry more passengers than all other methods combined, should also be automatically controlled.

Automatic highway systems were demonstrated in the United States in the late 1950s, and the technology has greatly improved since then. Short sections of test track have been built and proved viable. In the next phase, short sections of automated freeway will be built and traffic will begin to operate on them under the control of fast computer systems that regulate speed, the distance between vehicles, and even their entry and exit from the automated sections.

Are the advantages to such a system sufficient to make

drivers give up control of their vehicles to the computer? One point in favor of the idea is that the automatic highway should be safer than the present system. Today we have a great variety of drivers using the same highways. Some are young and eager; some are old and cautious. Many are in a hurry; others creep along. A few speed up, then slow down, and sometimes zigzag from one lane to another. There are those who are easily confused and get lost on freeways almost as soon as they enter them. And then there are the drunk drivers. All these problems could be solved by the automatic highway.

On our existing freeways, more cars per hour can pass a given point when traveling more slowly than the speed limit for the freeway. This is true because human drivers tend to leave more space between vehicles as they speed up—a precaution which is recommended. However, a computer-controlled system would eliminate the human lag and error and operate all cars at maximum safe speed. There would be no need for passing, since each car would travel at a fixed speed and maintain its distance from other vehicles. Automatic braking would be used in emergencies, should they develop.

The automated freeway could prevent the entry of the drunken driver, and the long-distance driver might safely rest during his trip and enjoy the trip along with his passengers, for changes of route could be programmed into the car's computer and made automatically at the proper place. Where some drivers are behind the wheel, this would mean that the passengers also would enjoy their trip more. Experts predict that one automated lane will handle the traffic of three or four lanes of normal freeway. It will permit faster speeds and safer driving, with accidents caused by human error all but eliminated. There would be no loss of control by dozing drivers, and no drunks smashing into other cars. Highway fatalities, many of which are believed to be actually suicides, would be practically impossible on a computer-controlled highway.

Smog would become a vague memory of the past. With silent electric motors instead of oil or gas burners, the air should be quiet and clean, and roadways would not be fouled with dripping fuels. There would be no fire hazard, and probably no stops necessary for fuel. Indeed, the electric car would cause a major change in the "filling station" as we know it. In its place might be a "quick-change station," repair shop and rest stop. We would probably be billed by computer for the electric power used by our vehicles on the automated highway.

If we are to use electric motors, of course electric power must be produced. Would this not produce just as much pollution in the long run? The answer, happily, is no. A conventional steam-electric plant or nuclear plant producing the power for 100,000 vehicles would produce far less pollution than these vehicles would separately, in addition to being more efficient in its conversion of fuel to power. Furthermore, what little pollution did result could be confined to a remote area where it would not be a nuisance and hazard to highway or city.

Potentialities for a personal-public transportation system like the one we have been describing are tremendous. The car of tomorrow would park in the garage just like present gasoline-engine cars. Its battery would be charged each night from the wall socket. Because battery-powered trips would be short, the battery need not be large. Thus the car could be of smaller and lighter construction than today's internal-combustion models. Local trips will be made with the flexibility we crave. Long trips can offer safety, economy, and speed. Hundred-mile-an-hour speeds are probable. Some of us have driven that fast on the freeways.

Swing onto the freeway in New York, set the controls on "Automatic" and punch San Francisco (with rest stops every few hours) into the route computer. In twenty-four hours' driving time, and seldom touching the controls, you are in San Francisco, having enjoyed the scenery, slept, read, played games and generally already started your vacation, while the computer did the driving!

Flying: The Fastest Way to Go

In 1950 airplanes carried less than 2 percent of intercity passenger traffic. By 1970 air travel accounted for more than 10 percent. Such an increase cannot continue, because automobile use will most likely not be reduced, but air travel should gain by one or two percentage points in the years ahead. We love the automobile, but we love to fly too. Speed is the overriding appeal, for time is a precious commodity. Not many years ago a vacation in Europe was almost unthinkable for many Americans, as was an American vacation for Europeans. Now it is possible to make the trip in just a few hours. A person with a two-week vacation can spend practically all of it abroad. So fast is air travel that many people even spend weekends thousands of miles from home.

The automatic highway will get us across the country in one day. An airliner presently does the job in about four hours, so we can make a round-trip by air across the country during the daylight hours. Few motorists can get far from home over a weekend, but the plane makes that possible. Supersonic airliners will make European weekends standard travel procedure, and two-week trips will be planned not just to Europe, but all around the world.

Let's start off on a smaller scale, however, and work up to the round-the-world jet slowly. The next generation will most probably not commute to school or work by helicopter or rocket belt. But air travel over very short distances will be much more common than it is now. New breeds of aircraft are beginning to make this possible already. Beginning with the helicopter, which can land and take off from a tiny heliport or helipad, the airlines are moving to STOL and VTOL designs.

With its propellers pointing skyward, this aircraft can take off and land vertically, making aerial transportation available to many more people.

These "short take-off" and "vertical take-off" craft will bring air service to the smallest community without the need for a large and expensive airport.

Early Florida legislation called for aircraft to fly as slowly as eight miles per hour when at low altitudes. Conventional aircraft would fall out of the sky at such speeds, but the new STOLS are able to move at speeds a fraction of the minimum speed of conventional types. There are now fighter planes capable of rising and descending vertically which can use tiny landing areas, but the noise of such craft is still a problem. If it can be tamed to an acceptable level, look for air travel hops as short as ten miles in busy city areas.

Ground transportation is limited to roads, but air transportation opens up an infinity of "roads" and also an infinity of "levels." Freeways have progressed to the point of using several levels of traffic at interchanges, but aircraft can be "stacked" as high as we want to go. This requires careful traffic control but it is obvious that many more airways exist over a given area than do highways.

It is barely possible that slow-flying VTOLs will make "personal flight" widespread. Even with the long trip to and from the airport, private aircraft are very popular and more people acquire them each year. If it were possible to operate "out of one's backyard," personal air travel would greatly increase. "Roadable" airplanes were built and flown years ago (some even suffered the embarrassment of running out of gas aloft) and the time may come when we have a convertible flivver-plane we can drive from home to a nearby take-off area. This however, is a possibility that already overworked air controllers prefer not to think about.

Large jetliners will continue to carry the bulk of domestic air traffic for some time to come. At scheduled speeds of ten miles a minute they link our coasts in four hours, and trips anywhere in the country are limited only by one's pocketbook. With more people, with more money to spend, air travel can only increase. This means that more airliners will be built and more pilots and other personnel will be employed. There may be setbacks, of course. As large craft carry greater passenger loads, and more of such craft are aloft, the dangers will increase. The collision of two jumbo jets is terrible to consider, yet 1,600 were killed in the *Titanic* disaster many decades ago and the disaster had little effect on ocean travel. Looking at it another way, while a few hundred may be killed in a year of air travel, nearly 60,000 now die on our highways in the same period.

It is possible that the SST will fly on America's airlines. Again, it is a question of speed. With a choice of getting to New York in four hours or two hours, most of us would take the shorter trip. Everyone wants to get there first.

Even 1,800 miles an hour may be only a beginning. The "hypersonic" transport mentioned earlier is not far behind on the drawing board; the X-15 rocket plane long ago demonstrated that flight faster than 4,000 miles an hour is feasible. Speed will continue to be the prize.

It may well be that by the end of this century an air traveler can be anywhere on earth in three hours. Even that speed has been exceeded by our astronauts, who orbit the planet in about 90 minutes. Except for the details of takeoff and landing, that is halfway around the earth in 45 minutes. It is hard to imagine needing more speed than that, but we shall see that someone has suggested a way to cut three minutes from that schedule.

SENTIMENTAL SEA JOURNEY

Although the automobile and the airplane will probably serve even larger numbers of travelers than they now do, other forms of transportation will not vanish. There will still be some passenger travel by water, although its share of the total will likely remain a tiny fraction of one percent.

Long ago, marine engineers seem to have reached a plateau in ship design. The transatlantic records set decades ago still stand, and it seems unlikely that conventional passenger liners will beat them, particularly since there is little passenger traffic on such runs anymore. The excursion ship is enjoying a new popularity, but whether that boom will continue is questionable. The U. S. government's experiment with nuclear power on the *U. S. S. Savannah* seems to have been a failure, and the dream of a ship steaming around the world many times without tons of fuel and even without refueling seems dead. There is a prospect for improvement in sea travel, however. It is called the "hovercraft."

A hovercraft making the transition from water to land. *Westland Aircraft Ltd.*

Developed in England, the hovercraft operates on a cushion of air several feet thick, eliminating the friction of water contact. It also eliminates the rough ride resulting from a choppy sea. A rather ungainly craft, and quite noisy, it offers water travel at about twice conventional speeds. There are many operating hovercraft, including a few in America that make short, highspeed runs. The hovercraft has the added advantage of not having to stop at the water's edge, since it can operate over land as well. Another innovation is the "hydrofoil," a craft that lifts itself out of the water and "planes" over the sea on thin foils that remain just below the surface. Such craft appear promising but have not yet had great commercial success.

As he has for many years, man still ventures *beneath* the sea as well. Submarine craft, dating back to Robert Fulton and earlier, have a long heritage as a mode of travel, and their use will doubtless continue in the future. Ranging in size from tiny one- and two-man research and exploration craft to giant nuclear-powered submarines, undersea craft may some day locate and mine rich deposits on and beneath the sea bottom, tend "herds" of fish raised as food, and provide fast and economical transportation for freight and passengers regardless of weather or sea conditions on the surface.

Submarine craft are at once exciting and dangerous means of transportation. Carrying their crews into an environment of strange beauty, undersea craft are also subjected to awesome forces of nature. Unfortunately, the result is too often a tragic accident taking the lives of bold explorers. We have much to learn about the depths of the sea, and the engineering of craft to operate in such conditions, before man can be as at home as he is in the more natural environment of Earth's surface.

There is little likelihood that ships will attain speeds of several hundred miles an hour, and just as little likelihood of their winning back any appreciable amount of passenger traffic to the oceans.

TRAINS AND MORE TRAINS

There will still be trains and buses, too, some of them improved dramatically to win passengers. Again, the appeal will be speed. The 170-mile-an-hour Turbo-Train is not even close to what the designers of high-speed trains have on the drawing board and even in test stages.

Years ago Ford experimented with its "Levatrain," a vehicle using rails but not wheels. For all its advantages, the wheel has limitations. For one thing it cannot hold together safely much beyond a few hundred miles an hour because of the great rotational stresses. Ford and other manufacturers have investigated the movement of heavy vehicles a fraction of an inch above the track on a thin film of air. Here was the old Stone Age sled carried to its extreme, with friction eliminated not by grease, water, or butter, but by air itself. In effect, the Levatrain was an airplane flying at extremely low altitude. Another experimental train is the French "Aerotrain." Much like the Levatrain, it has been tested at 215 miles an hour.

Since original experiments with the Levatrain, the "ground effect machine" has been developed extensively, as we saw elsewhere in this chapter. The ideas are similar, and yet the thin-film idea seems to hold the most promise. If offers the safety and security of rail travel plus relatively high speed. Research is now under way on trains of the future that will travel 250 to 300 miles an hour. Even such a 5-mile-a-minute speed is not enough, according to some Japanese scientists. For several years Professor Hisanojo Ozawa has been testing models of a wheelless train he designed, running on a cushion of air and propelled by jet engines. A full-size train would travel at more than 700 miles an hour.

Years ago department stores used to dispatch change, purchase orders, and other paperwork through pneumatic tubes. This quaint system is seldom seen anymore, but a variety of other products are still delivered in pipelines. Oil, gas, water, grain, and even concrete slurry are some of these. Imaginative engineers have proposed that people also can be transported in this way, and some interesting "tube trains" have been proposed. Engineer L. K. Edwards designed one that is a challenging concept. Fitting the tube tightly, it would be driven along by compressed air. The tube would descend abruptly on leaving a station, to add speed to the train, climbing again at the next station so that gravity would aid in slowing the train for a stop. Edwards predicted speeds of 500 miles an hour for his vehicle.

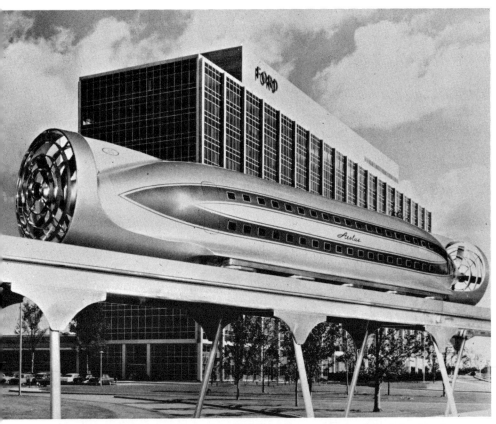

A wheelless vehicle similar to this 200-passenger scale model of the Ford Aeolus may some day provide fast intercity travel. *Ford Motor Company.*

More than a century ago Alfred Ely Beach, editor and publisher of *Scientific American*, built and operated a one-block-long stretch of "pneumatic subway." A huge fan drove a small cylindrical car back and forth in the tube, and Beach proved that his idea worked. However, except for limited use by the Post Office Department for handling mail, his clever method never caught on.

At first thought such a project promises to be ridiculously expensive, and it would indeed be costly. Edwards and his colleagues estimated a cost for the tunnel alone of about $5 million a mile. However, they also pointed out that a track like Japan's Tokkaido Line would cost about $6 million a mile in America, and a modern freeway can cost up to $18 million a mile.

Dr. Joseph V. Foa, of Rensellaer Polytechnic Institute, also has designed a tube train, although his would not be propelled by compressed air. Instead, it would take in air from ahead of it, burn it with fuel and eject the hot gas from the rear of the train for motive power. Foa calls his system "tube flight" and estimates speeds of 500 to 2,000 miles an hour.

ANYWHERE IN 42 MINUTES!

The "pendulum effect" of gravity for speeding and slowing down his train is a key part of Edwards' idea. There is an even more breathtaking application of this application of this principle. In 1966 Dr. Paul W. Cooper published a paper in the *American Journal of Physics* describing his idea for a "tunnel train" system linking major cities all over the world. The train would use gravity as its major power source.

In the Cooper system, a tunnel would be dug connecting two cities. For travel between Boston and Washington, the tunnel woud be five miles deep. Leaving the station, the train would accelerate rapidly as it "fell" through the tunnel, continuing to increase in speed until it passed the low point at the middle of the run. Then the train would gradually decelerate until it reached its destination. Elapsed time? A startling 42.2 minutes. Even more remarkable, travel between even the most distant cities of the earth would still take only 42.2 minutes! This is because of the basic principle of the system, and the fact that the longer trip would build up faster speeds. Cooper's system would provide travel halfway around the earth faster than an orbiting spacecraft moving at 18,000 miles an hour.

Cooper is first to point out that a great many problems stand in the way of such tunnel travel, among them the mechanics of boring the tunnel. However, his kind of trans-

An artist's conception of the tube train driven by compressed air within a clear plastic tube.

portation would have many things in its favor. It would be completely independent of weather, use no fuel, produce no pollution, and require no surface right of way. And its speed would be unmatched, of course.

It would be best not to make any bets on being able to travel to anywhere in 42 minutes by train, or even in 3 hours by hypersonic transport. Such high-speed transportation may come in a few decades or it may never come at all. We must wait and see. The same condition applies to the prospect of pleasure trips to the moon, monorails for urban transit, and personal helicopters atop each garage. These are fine details we can only guess at, knowing that the guesses will probably be wrong. However, the broad outline of travel in the future can be made out without the need for a crystal ball. We have tried to do that in this book, using the past, the present, and common sense. No matter how we travel, or how much it is improved over the methods we know today, it is assured that man will continue to be in rapid motion. It is our heritage as active, curious creatures, fortunate to be born in a world so large and so interesting to explore.

Bibliography

Bray, Peter & Brown, Barbara. *Transport Through the Ages*. New York, Taplinger, 1971

Burby, John. *Great American Motion Sickness; Or Why You Can't Get There From Here*. Boston, Little Brown, 1971

Danforth, Paul. *Transportation; Managing Man on the Move*. New York, Doubleday, 1970.

Dietz, Betty W. *You Can Work in the Transportation Industry*. John Day, 1969

Duche, Jean. *Great Trade Routes*. New York, McGraw-Hill, 1969

Freeman, Dorothy R. *Very Important People Who Work with Cars, Buses & Trucks*. New York, Children's Press, 1968

Gray, Genevieve S. *Jobs In Transportation*. New York, Lothrop, Lee, & Shepard, 1973

Halacy, Daniel S. Jr. *The Shipbuilders*, Philadelphia, Lippincott, 1966
———— *33 Miles A Minute! The Story of Air Transport*. New York, Messner, 1966

Hellman, Hal. *Transportation in the World of the Future*. New York, M. Evans, 1968

Hornung, Clarence P. *Wheels Across America*. New York, A. S. Barnes,

James, Leonard F. *Following the Frontier: American Transportation in the Nineteenth Century*. New York, Harcourt Brace, 1968

141

Lee, Laurie, & Lambert, David. *Wonderful World of Transportation. New York, Doubleday, 1970*

Lewellen, John. *You and Transportation.* New York, Children's Press, 1965

McLeod, Sterling. *How Will We Move All the People: Transportation for Tomorrow's World.* New York, Messner, 1971

Ross, Frank, Jr. *Transportation of Tomorrow.* New York, Lothrop, Lee & Shepard, 1968

Index

143

146

147

Pyramids of Egypt, 25

Queen Mary, S. S., 63, 122
Quimby, Harriet, 95-96

Rafts, 13, 53
Railroad bridges, collapse of, 71
Railroad gauges, 66-67
Railroads
  vs. airlines, 74-75
  Amtrak and, 77-78
  automobile and, 75
  bankruptcy of, 77-78
  decline of, 73-75
  development of, 42-45
  first U. S., 64
  freight business of, 77
  future of, 135-138
  growth of, 64-78
  hundred-mile-an-hour, 75-76
  narrow-gauge, 67
  passenger traffic and, 125-126
  safety and, 71-72
  speed records of, 72-73, 136-137
  "supertrain" and, 75-77
  track mileage of, 5, 72
  transcontinental, 68-71
  vs. trucks, 77
  World War II and, 73-74
  see also Locomotive; Trains
Ra raft, 53
Red Sea, 58
Reeds, as raft, 13
Reindeer, 16
Rex, S. S., 63
Rickenbacker, Eddie, 97
Rickett, Thomas, 46
Rickshaw, 34
Right-hand driving, 33
Rivers, mileage of, 6
Roadable airplanes, 132
Roads
  communication and, 31
  driving on left or right side of, 33
  early, 28-32
  European, 33-34
  night driving on, 34
  passenger traffic and, 34
  primitive, 20

Roman Empire and, 30-31
  see also Highways
Rocket belt, 103
Rocket locomotive, 71
Rockets, Chinese, 92
Rogers, Will, 98
Roller, wheel and, 25
Roman bridges, 31
Roman roads, 30-33
  traffic problems on, 32
  women chariot drivers on, 32
Rotary engine, 51
Royal William, Atlantic crossing by, 61
Rozier, M. de, 93
Ruskin, John, 75

Safety bicycles, 36
Sailboats, 14, 24, 41
Sailors, ancient, 12-14, 52
Sailplanes, 103-105
San Francisco, BART system in, 119-120
Savannah, U.S.S., 61, 133
Savery, Thomas, 39
Scientific American, 81, 137
Scuba outfit, primitive, 13
Sea lanes, 53-55
Sea power, waning of, 63
Seattle *Post-Intelligencer*, 107
Selfridge, Lt. Thomas E., 95
Serpollet, Leon, 46-48
Shanghaiing, practice of, 55
Sheep, domesticating of, 16
Shipbuilding, 53
Ships
  future of, 133-135
  number of, 6
  see also Sailboats; Steamships; Submarines
Shooting Star airplane, 100-101
Skis, 20-21
Skyjacking, 103
Slavery, ships and, 54, 56
Sledges, 20-21, 24
Smog, 126, 129
Solar cells, 87
Solar heat, 37
Sonic boom 107
Sound barrier, 105-108
South Carolina Railroad, 66

150